Selected Themes in Nursing Home Management

Selected Themes in Nursing Home Management

A CNA's Critique

EDWIN A. NGERI

authorHOUSE®

AuthorHouse™
1663 Liberty Drive
Bloomington, IN 47403
www.authorhouse.com
Phone: 1-800-839-8640

© 2012 by Edwin A. Ngeri. All rights reserved.

No part of this book may be reproduced, stored in a retrieval system, or transmitted by any means without the written permission of the author.

Published by AuthorHouse   10/16/2012

ISBN: 978-1-4772-7983-0 (sc)
ISBN: 978-1-4772-7981-6 (hc)
ISBN: 978-1-4772-7982-3 (e)

Library of Congress Control Number: 2012919189

Any people depicted in stock imagery provided by Thinkstock are models, and such images are being used for illustrative purposes only.
Certain stock imagery © Thinkstock.

This book is printed on acid-free paper.

Because of the dynamic nature of the Internet, any web addresses or links contained in this book may have changed since publication and may no longer be valid. The views expressed in this work are solely those of the author and do not necessarily reflect the views of the publisher, and the publisher hereby disclaims any responsibility for them.

Executives are constrained not by resources but by their imagination.

                                        C. K. Prahalad
                                        1941-2010

Contents

Dedication ix

Acknowledgement xi

Introduction.. xv

List of Abbreviations and Meanings............................. xix

Chapter One: The Nursing Home 1

Chapter Two: Resident Rights and Care Delivery 14

Chapter Three: Difficult Residents and Difficult Family Members 41

Chapter Four: Diversity Management: The African-Born CNA 67

Chapter Five: A Model for Nursing Home Management... 95

Bibliography/References 121

Dedication

To late Perry A. Ngeri, my beloved brother who passed to the great beyond on the 6th of September, 2012—as I was putting finishing touches to this work. Even as I type the lines on this page I cannot help but wonder why you did not wait a bit longer to see your brother's first book. I take condolence in the fact that He, who gave you life, has called you to a better place. Perry, may your gentle soul rest in the Lord's bosom. Adieu, my brother.

Also to all the hardworking nursing assistants in the United States, especially those who work in the nursing home environment, may you be rewarded by competitive America for the great job you do. Enough love to all of you.

Acknowledgement

Even a book, as small as this one is did not just come to be by the dual efforts of the author, and the publishers. True, I spent so many days and nights, pounding on the keyboard of my laptop computer to put down the content here-in, and communicating with the publishers to make the book a reality, this reality would probably still be elusive without the formidable support I enjoyed from family and friends chosen by my creator for this purpose. I thank God almighty, for the unmerited gift of a purposeful life, which only partly manifests here in the form of knowledge gained through education.

To my wife, Mrs Toni Edwin-Ngeri, and children, Mudiaga, Ayebaifie, and Jacqueline, I am not unaware of the real price you paid as I stubbornly went after my pursuits. I may have, timely, fallen short of your collective expectations of me, both as a husband, and a daddy, but it is my assurance to you, that though popular eyes and ears could not have seen or heard what I saw and heard, I saw clearly, and listened attentively, as they were designed for my eyes and ears. At the appropriate time, He, who showed me what I saw, and spoke the words I heard, will cause these to manifest upon your lives. I truly love you all.

To Boma Iruene, and Walkie Cheah; a true brother, and a true sister, you were called to be to me, I cannot stop thanking God for knowing you. Katrina Lavette Sweet, meeting you at the Capella doctoral classes was awesome, but with **Silent Screams** you have remained a wonderful source of inspiration. To Emmanuel Ebitimi George, who saw the vision of my writing a book, in 2002, I thank you so much. I could not have talked about team work, in this book, without the live lessons learnt from working with Dauda and Katrina Parks. To say we were the greatest team in the block, at the time, is only stating an objective truth.

To Irigha J. Obuala, Emmanuel Young, and Victor Clement, I feel humbled by the magnitude of your belief in me, especially in recent times when holding on became really challenging for me. I wholeheartedly appreciate your unrelenting support. I am also thankful to Akpos, Alfani, Thomas, Udeh, Ikiogha, Barine, Alanso, Lucky Nwosu, Lucky, Manny, Ayebaemi, Ebinyo, Pastor Levi, Evangelist

Ike, Lemlem, Amadi, Aye, Idowu, Madam Helena Olotu Asu, Emmanuel & Gifty, and Paul & Lori Hinton, for your thoughtfulness.

To Madam Juliana Ogobiri, my lovely mother, I will ever remain grateful to God for choosing you to be my mom. I cannot thank you enough. And to all my brothers and sisters, though your brother may be separated from you, by distance, I daily live with you mentally and spiritually, especially at this time when we collectively mourn our late brother, Perry. Finally, to my extended family of nursing assistants and nurses, I salute you all.

May God bless all of you, including those others that, space, memory, and time will not permit me to mention here. It is my prayer that HE raises men and women to support you, at your times of need.

Introduction

According to a 2004, National Nursing Home Survey report, 16, 100 nursing homes existed, in the United States of America. These nursing homes held a collective capacity of 1.7million beds, though actual occupancy was 1.5 million, at the time. Since then, various performance evaluation surveys on nursing homes classified these nursing homes into five stars, four stars, three stars, two stars, and one star categories, based on yardsticks used by the evaluators. Amongst other findings, performance surveys showed, by their ratings, that some nursing homes did perform better than others, as if, that by itself is anything out of the usual. Outperformance, whether by an organization or an individual, over a counterpart is most often linked to resource differentials (especially the combination and deployment) between the outperformer, and the underperformer. What the performance evaluation report and other similar reports may very well shy away from is, whether or if, even the best practices of the five star earning nursing homes truly approximate well defined and broad based expectations of how care providing facilities should cater for the elder, frail, and most likely totally dependent member of society, especially that of a modern society.

In this small-sized book, I present the perspective that the nursing home is still far away from even the ideals they profess to uphold. Armed with an almost ten-year experience of running around the floors of nursing homes providing direct care services to elder residents, I reason that the gap between the present state of nursing homes, and the desired end state, as far as meeting what is expected of them, could be explained from some deep-seated managerial practices. At the core of such practices, in my view, is the popular CNA to residents' ratio which ranges from an aide to eight or ten residents. I throw my weight around a thought frame that unless nursing homes effectively manage the primary core care giver, the certified nursing assistant, the end state which they desire will continue to remain a mirage.

Based on my experience, I have selected a few themes that have direct bearing on the daily life of a nursing home and its residents. My approach is to start with definitional bases of the chosen themes as they relate to the nursing home environment, from where I move to presentations of practices extant in nursing homes. I conclude on each theme by critically examining what nursing homes do, and providing recommendations for improvement. And of course, for better understanding, I have provided some 'real time' scenarios to drive home my message. For style, the content of this book, is delivered in a mixture of high critical fervor, and my sense of cutting edge humor; the former representing the depth of anomalies in nursing homes and the need for urgency to reverse same, while the latter communicates the need to loosen up and smile, to serving nursing assistants as they continue in their most challenging and frustrating roles, in the nursing home.

Amidst teary eyes from nurses and CNAs, as they struggled to give their last hugs and messages of goodwill, on the last day I worked as a full time nursing assistant, in the nursing home, I had taken a quiet look at them, especially those that pleaded that I stayed back, temporarily bitter that I was leaving them after this length of stay, and the only thing I can remember telling them was, "I need to leave for now, so that when I return the nursing home will be a better place to work". This book signifies not only my return, but also the beginning of my contributory efforts towards making the nursing home a better place both for staff and residents. The last theme, 'A Model for Nursing Home Management', lays out the architectural work.

Edwin A. Ngeri

List of Abbreviations and Meanings

NAR Nursing Assistant, registered

CNA Certified Nursing Assistant

PCA Personal Care Assistant

HHA Home Health Aide

TMA Trained Medication Assistant

LPN Licensed Practicing Nurse

RN   Registered Nurse

DON Director of Nursing

ADL Activities of Daily Living such as dressing, bathing, feeding, toileting, and transfers

Chapter One

THE NURSING HOME

Because this book is about aspects of nursing homes' management, it wouldn't be a bad idea to start with an introductory chapter that draws one closer to the internal environment of a seemingly well-known organization. After all unrealizable expectations are placed routinely on this organization. Even for the insider or nursing home veteran, the perspectives offered in this book may provoke a rethinking of some of the old practices that have characterized the nursing home. For one thing, there is no dispute that the nursing home was created to cater to society's aging population, especially those whose families would find it most challenging to provide care. For example, coping with the daily complexities of providing a living for themselves while attending (twenty-four hours per day) to an aged family member would make providing care quite hard. According to a national nursing home survey conducted in 2004, there were 16,100 nursing homes with 1.7 million beds in the United States. The real occupancy rate, though, was said to be at 86 percent, bringing total occupancy to 1.5 million. With the future senior population projected to rise, it is only reasonable to expect that the number of seniors in need of the services presently provided by nursing homes will also increase.

An important point of consideration—not only for nursing homes but also for the future seniors and their family members—is whether future demand for elder-care services will lean more toward other parallel arrangements. These arrangements might include home health care and assisted living providers or the traditional nursing home. It is true that far less than half of the population over sixty-five who need some form of elder-care service lives in a traditional nursing home facility. The larger part of this population is distributed among assisted living facilities and varying forms of senior living arrangements. There are still others who live in their own homes or with family members. In all of the latter arrangements (and depending on need), direct care providers such as personal care assistants (PCAs), and home health aides (HHAs) are contracted to provide needed services. Smith and Baughman (2007, p25) observed that home health aide and home care aide were the "fastest-growing occupations," a trend they believed would continue.

It may not be entirely wrong to reason (at this point) that the current market share of traditional nursing homes in the elder-care services broader market will likely contract as demand rises in the future. This will not be due to existing limitations of traditional nursing homes—as far as number, size, and bed space—when compared to all other non-nursing home elder-care providers. Rather, this contraction will be due to the nursing home model of caring for the elderly. Interestingly, nursing homes are not unaware of this fact; there have been talks about reinventing the nursing home. Some nursing homes have commenced internal remodeling, acquired furniture, and installed new equipment. Others have had to put up brand new structures. Sometimes, the temptation to use phrases such as "the new nursing home," and "neighborhood community" only end up masking the reality of the so-called refurbished nursing home. This linguistic hijacking is ubiquitous. Like some churchgoers who speak in fake tongues (both old and new), nursing homes *promote innovation, workplace diversity, and employee excellence.* Plus, they are all *customer-centric.* Like the average MBA from any American university, these nursing homes possess *cutting-edge* solutions to all resident needs and problems. As the popular saying goes, "A pig remains a pig." And the "new" nursing homes remain stuck in the old ways of the old nursing homes—ways that have worked against the whole idea of caring for the elderly. I will describe some fundamental aspects of the nursing home model—aspects that run counter to avowed claims.

The Nursing Home Model

By *nursing home model*, I refer to the arrangements put in place by nursing home management to provide activities of daily living (ADLs) for residents or clients. ADLs include assistance with bathing, clothing, feeding, transferring, and toileting—activities that are vital for the smooth functioning of nursing home residents. These are activities for which over 90 percent of nursing home residents depend wholly on certified nursing assistants for assistance. For many of the residents, the inability to perform ADLs on their own accounts overwhelmingly for their residency in long-term care-giving facilities. Some of the ADLs run on predetermined schedules, but whenever residents and their family members evoke the popular needs-and-rights argument, such schedules either totally give way or get modified. For nursing homes' management, the standard is that of zero-tolerance for an aide not assisting residents with ADLs. All residents must be continuously (for the duration of the aide's shift) assisted whenever a resident says, "It's time." Anyone who knows anything about input-output relationships will be getting ready to ask one question: How does a nursing home allocate aides (certified nursing assistants, CNAs) to residents in a way that will sufficiently meet the residents' ADL needs and other management-assigned responsibilities for aides?

The typical ratio in most nursing homes is one CNA to eight residents. There are facilities where an aide gets up to ten residents. These numbers also increase when an aide calls in and is not replaced by management. The residents are often categorized into units and assigned to an aide at the start of a shift. CNAs are traditionally responsible for assisting residents in their units with all the activities of daily living as stated in respective assignment/unit sheets. Also, all aides on a floor during a particular shift are held liable for not attending to requests from residents who are not in their units. Nursing home residents are not necessarily homogeneous in character and behavior. They are senior adult members of society, most of whom were raised in an individualistic culture and legally empowered to so act. The demands and requests they make on a CNA are mainly self-centered. They do not have to depend on the feelings or demands of fellow residents assigned to the same CNA.

Another aspect of the nursing home model is the inadequacy of equipment and supplies at the time of need. It is common practice for CNAs to spend ample productive time in search of needed equipment to assist with the transfer of a resident (or to get needed supplies that should always be in a resident's corner). Sometimes, aides have to go as far as other floors to get an EZ-stand, a sling, or an adult diaper. One wonders what this would mean to a surgeon if the latter had to leave the surgery room three to four times to fetch needed instruments for an operation. Maybe it makes good management sense for a gynecologist to spend an hour or two fetching necessary items for a C-section procedure that will only take twenty-five minutes. If the standard 1:8 or 1:10 aide to residents ratio causes you to doubt nursing homes' claims that they provide quality care to almost totally dependent senior adult citizens, be prepared to become more skeptical. The equipment and supplies shortage makes one wonder whether such nursing homes really care for their residents.

As will be seen in the next chapter, nursing homes are supposed to be protecting all residents' rights, which include that of eating at any time. Dietary services and times are centralized for all residents in most nursing homes. This makes it mandatory for residents to eat at prescheduled times because dietary services close for the day at about 7 p.m. in most nursing homes. These circumstances do not allow the residents to fully exercise their fundamental rights. What is often left in resident dining rooms is limited to bread and cereal. Nursing home residents are not normally allowed enough time to eat and enjoy their meals because dietary aides need to leave in a hurry to perform some other necessary tasks in the kitchen, or because assigned aides have to be in other places at the same time. Nursing home managers appear to be saying one thing and doing another. In sum, the nursing home does not look capable of caring for helpless residents.

When contrasted with residents in other elder-care services arrangements—such as assisted living and group homes—nursing home residents are usually more dependent on their direct-care primary provider, the CNA. This level of dependence, given the age and physiological condition of the nursing home resident, requires the CNA to dedicate himself or herself to the residents and provide ample time to each resident. The resident is not supposed to be hustled, jostled, and rushed as he or she is cared for. Even an idiot who works with a frail and old person knows this. Unfortunately, the nursing home model of primary care delivery as seen in the 1:8 CNA to residents' ratio more than compulsively redirects the CNA from this noble path. A CNA literally juggles between and among residents to get his or her job done. Like the conveyor belt (which stops only for maintenance), the CNA cannot spend much time with one resident without spending less with another. Aside from continuous lecturing (called training and education), nursing homes have no structural alternatives. CNAs must adopt either the *fast food* or *work smart* approach. In either of these approaches, total quality care for residents is compromised.

The last—and perhaps the most important—component of the nursing home model is the role of management. In addition to the already-discussed aspects, which also call for a reevaluation and improvement of the role of management in nursing homes another matter must be considered. Management's treatment of variables such as staff professionalism, employee motivation, stress management, employee retention, diversity management, work culture, customer service, and relationships with CNAs need to be better addressed. For instance, does a nurse get hired because he or she possesses state-required qualifications and there is a shortage of nurses in the United States? Can every CNA on a particular floor function as a CNA on another floor? Is human resources management equal to hiring and firing, completion of benefit forms, and filling in missing spots on schedules? What happens when a CNA is repeatedly told to smile at residents, but the only time he or she is privy to a smile by the trainer is when the department of health surveyors are around? Is customer service as simple as telling a resident to pull the call light (even though there are no corresponding structures for immediate response)? If a registered nurse (RN) is qualified to become a director of nursing, does that mean he or she can run a nursing home?

Nursing homes have continued to exist in great numbers—even though many of them suffer from the shortcomings just described. True, some of them (probably a handful), have done better. Still, the continued existence of the majority of these nursing homes (especially those classified as non-profit organizations) is not due to their excellence. Rather, it is because they enjoy free financing, consumers' fear of the temporary increased price that will be charged if nursing home services are provided entirely by profit-seeking organizations, and the normalization of fundamental practices by appropriate authorities. The assertion, however, is not that for-profit nursing homes have overwhelmingly done better. The point is that there is so much wastage in nursing homes that are owned and operated by so-called non-profit organizations. This wastage has its roots in the misunderstanding of management about its function in an organization, especially as time changes.

This basic flaw in not understanding the management function manifests in faulty recruitment of line and supervisory staff, misalignment of organizational goals, unrealistic target setting and expectations, and lack of recognition for CNAs as key implementers of care delivery programs. For instance, what corporate-level or facility-level management personnel determine (and on what basis) that one CNA can effectively provide care for eight or ten wholly dependent, frail, and (often) very slow residents? It has never worked, and never will! And where is the department of health surveyor who accepts this 1:8 formula as immutable only to make a note on those paper files (fit for the shredder) that CNAs need to respond promptly to call lights. If the department of health surveyor previously worked as an aide in 1970 and had to assist with ADLs for twenty residents, he or she can also tell us the number of law firms that handled resident abuse cases in 1970. And then he or she can compare that number to the number of cases in 2012.

I am not ignorant of the concept of cost-effective staffing. I do not have a black belt in six-sigma, I never worked for Motorola, and I couldn't easily recognize Jack Welsh if I walked past him. I respect his unassailable record and contributions—not only to GE, but also to modern management thinking. I know that some activities and processes (even in the nursing home) can be streamlined. Nevertheless, I also know that, though we live in a world of technological wonders, we are still far away from developing process streamlining efforts that effectively time how long a seventy-five-year-old resident requires for a particular ADL.

Where cost-effective staffing is based on an organization's clearly determined priorities, the provision of ADLs for residents should top the list for nursing homes. It is silly to make an aide care for eight or ten residents while so many paper-pushing employees roam around the offices and corridors of nursing homes. On the other hand, if management learns that there are CNAs who can accomplish these tasks (maybe on Mars or Jupiter), nothing should stop management from hiring them. To assume that, because CNAs on Mars can function at a certain level, CNAs on Earth should be able to do the same—that idea is even more outrageous. It is akin to thinking that Apple Inc. can hire any computer science graduate and charge him or her with the responsibility of developing the next iPad.

The Future of Nursing Homes and Elder-Care Services

If the preceding discussion on the nursing home model is anything to go by, it becomes clear that the nursing home faces a huge challenge of attracting the future consumer of elder-care services. Today's consumers are allegedly better informed than consumers of yesteryear, and future consumers will be even more informed than today's consumers. These future consumers will enjoy the benefit of pulling up information about elder-care service providers—including nursing homes—and making logical choices. The nursing home may not be competitive enough, and it may lag behind other elder-care service providers. Yet, it may have a place in the future. To the extent that competition finds its way into the business of elder-care services, providers may begin to specialize in catering for niche clientele. Depending, again, on the nature of the competition, nursing homes may retain those residents who have dementia or require more than one aide for assistance. Meanwhile, other providers will compete for what would appear as corporate clients—the aged new-schoolers. In a worst-case scenario, the number of nursing homes may be adversely affected by this competition.

Certainly, there are structural impediments the nursing home must address. Small and uncomfortable bedrooms—often with wheelchair inaccessible bathrooms—dorm-like dining rooms, the queuing up of residents in hallways like they are waiting to see a welfare officer . . . these are considerable problems. For the non-profit nursing home, the complaint is always that of inadequate funding. As managers of nursing homes continue to view these impediments as both the causes and effects of their ineffectiveness, they absolve themselves of their paid-for responsibilities. It is possible that Prahalad, the late professor of management, did not live long enough to teach today's nursing home managers a thing or two. Managers must learn that an organization is not constrained any more by its lack of resources than it is by its managers' lack of imaginativeness (Prahalad cited in Berfield 2010). For the nursing home of the future to be successful, managers must learn these lessons and effectively implement them.

Chapter Two

RESIDENT RIGHTS AND CARE DELIVERY

The nursing home, like any other organization that functions in a geo-political environment, has its fair share of regulatory authorities. The main regulatory authority is the relevant state department of health. A given department of health seeks to control—through the use of various instruments—the internal operational environment of the nursing home. Though its principal responsibility is to wring compliance from nursing homes' management, the state department of health does not create a manual of operations for the daily activities of management, employees, and residents of a nursing home. It remains the duty of the management of a nursing home to daily create and recreate an internal operating environment. The set of activities and complementary *modus operandi* capable of meeting the health department's laudable expectations must be established.

This theme—resident rights and cares delivery—points to three very important legal planks that govern the care-delivering activities of primary care-givers in a nursing home setting: the resident bill of rights, the vulnerable adult act, and the elder justice act. Traditionally, the resident bill of rights is posted in every nook and cranny within the living areas of nursing home residents. All residents, prior to their residency, are well informed of their rights. To the nursing assistant (the primary caregiver) with only a year on the job, the frequency with which training sessions on the vulnerable adult act are held is very high. In fact, it could equal the frequency that children watch *Diego* on television, on one hand, and the fervor with which Jesus Christ taught sermons on the mount, on the other. It is believed that the elder justice act will soon assume the status of the vulnerable adult act.

Despite the amount of time spent by managers of nursing homes to publicize these rights and acts, implementation could be greatly improved. The position here is not that nursing assistants have not been reported or fired enough by nursing home managers. Rather, problems arise when managers do not understand applicable statutes and deny their role in effectively creating the proper operating environment.

The Residents' Bill of Rights

The residents' bill of rights refers to the rights granted to all residents of nursing homes, boarding care homes, and other extended care facilities (MDH, 2007). Such rights derive from both federal and state laws. This means that, though the federally articulated rights may be the same for residents in all the states, each state can add to the list. This may give rise to slight differences in content from one state to another. This book ignores such differences because it does not intend to compare the rights of residents across the different states in the United States. Rather, it dwells on the managerial aspect of creating the necessary elder-friendly environment that will allow residents to enjoy such rights.

The rights contained in the Minnesota Department of Health (MDH pdf 2007), titled "Your Rights under the Combined Federal and Minnesota Residents Bill of Rights" is hereby adopted and referred to as the residents' bill of rights. The residents' bill of rights is a long list of forty-two rights broadly divided into five categories. The categories are as follows:

Quality of Life: This portion requires that resident must be cared for "in a manner and environment" consistent with both the sustenance and/or improvement of the resident's total quality of life. Specifically, the rights under this classification seek to promote the resident's dignity, self-determination, participation in resident and family groups and other activities, and personal needs.

Care and Treatment: This category deals with the resident's involvement in his or her care, treatment, and entitlements. The rights in question cover issues such as appropriate health care, relationships with other health services and suppliers, continuity of care, review of records, knowledge of care, advance directives, treatment information, participation in planning treatment, notice of changes in condition, refusal of treatment, and self-administration of drugs.

General Rights: The rights listed under this category seem to be anchored in the idea that the resident is a member of a modern, civil society. Therefore, he or she deserves a corresponding level of courteous and respectful treatment. These rights are as follows: exercise of rights, personal privacy, receipt of rights (not later than the time of admission), information about Medicaid and Medicare, notice of potential loss of Medicaid eligibility, personal funds, experimental research, change in room or roommate, confidentiality of records, expression of grievances, responsive service, examination of survey results, refusal to work for the facility, receiving and sending mail, access and visitation rights, communication privacy, access to a telephone and personal property, and the right to a marital relationship.

Resident Behavior and Facility Practices: To further promote the resident's right to a dignified lifestyle in a board-and-care nursing facility, a set of rights were added to the residents' repertoire. Basically, these rights address the very fundamental problem of resident abuse. Listed in the residents' bill of rights are the right to be free from all forms of restraint, the right to request and consent to a physical restraint, the right to be free from all forms of abuse, and the right to reprisals in the form of investigation and correction where abuse is suspected or inexplicable injuries are detected.

Admission, Transfer, and Discharge Rights: Once admitted, residents of nursing facilities cannot be transferred or discharged randomly. The decision to transfer or discharge a resident must be in compliance with the resident's rights (such as the refusal to transfer or discharge, an official statement to contest such a transfer or discharge, notice of bed-hold policy and readmission, and equal access to quality care).

These categories summarily describe the residents' bill of rights—a long list of resident rights that the nursing home must comply with (because these rights are derived from existing legal statutes). These rights are, therefore, laws. Given that rights and laws are often couched in the realm of ideals, the vulnerable adult act is very important. It does a good job at not only reducing ambiguity in the residents' bill of rights, but also at defining concrete actions to be taken if the dream behind the bill of rights is to be realized. The next section takes a look at the vulnerable adult act.

The Vulnerable Adult Act

Though the specifics as to what led to the promulgation of the vulnerable act may be variously stated, there exists the common ground that the act was predated by the mistreatment of a resident in a nursing home environment. Assuming full legal force in 1981, the vulnerable adult act sought (and still seeks) to provide a "living and care-giving" environment for adults not capable of protecting themselves. The law emphasizes (with respect to any incident of maltreatment), four important requirements: reporting, investigating, findings, and corrective and protective actions. Generally, the law has three key features, which I outline here:

Mandatory Reporting and Timelines: The vulnerable adult act requires the reporting of all cases of suspected and real maltreatments of vulnerable adults within twenty-four hours from the incident. It also designates all licensed health and human services professionals, direct care providers (such as CNAs and PCAs), and employees of licensed facilities as mandated reporters. This means that these categories of personnel must report both suspected and real cases of vulnerable adult maltreatment. Others not designated by the law may voluntarily report observed cases of resident maltreatment.

The Common Entry Point (CEP): Mainly defined by respective counties (in the state of Minnesota), the common entry point is an office, often outside of the facility, where all cases of vulnerable adult maltreatments must be reported. This is irrespective of whether or not an internal (within the facility) report has been made by a mandated reporter.

Abuse: In one simple sentence, the vulnerable adult act, with its aim of reporting resident maltreatment, can be viewed as a public policy purposed to prevent resident abuse. Federal law defines abuse as "The willful infliction of injury, unreasonable confinement, intimidation, or punishment with resulting physical harm, pain or mental anguish" (42 C. F. R.

488.301). The appropriate Minnesota statute refers to abuse as "Conduct which is not an accident or therapeutic." From these definitions, the vulnerable adult act recognizes abuse in varying forms: physical, emotional, sexual, financial, and verbal. Involuntary seclusion and neglect are also recognized. And all forms must be timely reported.

The Elder Justice Act

The elder justice act, passed in 2010, is a federal law that came as a response to a heightened public call for a national effort to address the problem of elder abuse in the United States (in the face of mounting statistics). Such statistics did not only point to the increasing rate of elder abuse, they also highlighted the fact that there was an underreporting epidemic. Other than elevating the issue of elder abuse to the level of child abuse and domestic violence, the elder justice act is not fundamentally different from the vulnerable adult act. At the nursing home level, however, management is required to conduct a national criminal background check on all potential employees. Again, mandated reporters, in addition to completing the reporting procedures under the vulnerable adult act, are also required to call a local police office to report suspected criminal acts against any resident.

The regulatory statutes just examined clearly point to the one goal of providing a live-in-and-cared-for environment for the elderly. They must be free from all conceivable forms of maltreatment. It is now time to take a look at what nursing homes do to realize this goal, especially as required by these statutes.

The Nursing Home in Action

As was mentioned earlier, the residents' bill of rights is generally posted in all open areas of nursing homes. It is equally true to say that both residents and their family members are properly informed of these rights before admission. It is hardly surprising to hear a new resident (a few days after admission) yell out, "It is my right! I am paying for this service!" In fact, the bill of rights constitutes an integral part of all training sessions in nursing homes. It is the practice, also, for nursing homes to conduct pre-employment background checks on prospective employees. In some cases, pre-employment drug and alcohol abuse tests are carried out. Those who are to provide services that require licensure are thoroughly investigated to ensure they are qualified.

Due to the importance of the residents' bill of rights and the far-reaching definition of the word *abuse* by the vulnerable adult act, any act of noncompliance with or denial of any of rights amounts to an abuse of some sort. This informs the degree of seriousness with which nursing homes facilitate training sessions on the vulnerable adult act. A typical training session commences with a refresher on the residents' bill of rights and gradually progresses to a definition of abuse. Finally, the different types of abusive behavior are outlined. Often, the facilitator provides scenarios to illustrate abusive behavior. It is not uncommon in these sessions for the facilitator to mention a widely publicized case in which a nursing assistant or nurse lost his or her license due to abuse-related conduct. Questions from participants are taken, and then some true-or-false testing takes place. Other training sessions on topics such as understanding difficult residents and customer service serve as boosters to the training on vulnerable adult act.

Though these training sessions are always mandatory, for all facility employees (and held in a classroom setting), for nursing assistants working on the floor, the vulnerable adult act training could be an everyday affair. The frequency of encounter depends on the shift (a.m., p.m., or night) and the number of non-aide facility employees likely to walk through the floor. The floor training sessions are mainly informal and devoid of clearly defined content. The training is delivered in a variety of ways—for example, micromanagement or talking down to the nursing assistant. The intent, irrespective of the mode of delivery, is to make the aide's behavior conform to the broad expectations of the vulnerable adult act.

To complement the ubiquitous formal and informal training sessions, managers of nursing homes utilize avenues such as staff meetings and care conferences. These meetings reiterate the need for in-house primary caregivers (nurses and nurses' aides) to comply with the standards set by both the residents' bill of rights and the vulnerable adult act. Though the frequency with which care conferences are held will put the nursing home well ahead of any known Fortune 500 company, staff meetings are need-based. And of course, adult residents and their family members never run out of complaints—a situation that calls for regular staff meetings.

Nursing home managers continue to spin the wheel of hiring and firing or firing and hiring. Typically preceded by a series of write-ups (warranted and unwarranted), management terminates the employment of an erring staff member. In this instance, management is supported by relevant sections of labor laws but not required to rationalize such acts. That management believes a nursing assistant's conduct can undermine stipulations of the residents' bill of rights and the vulnerable adult act is enough. Sometimes, statements such as "the front door is open" and "if this is not the place for you" are used to drive home the point that if a subordinate wants to remain an employee of the facility, he or she *must* do what is asked of him or her.

Up to this point, this work has looked at three important legal frameworks that collectively seek to define the operational climate of nursing homes. Also covered are the fundamentals of what nursing homes have done to create an ideal operational environment. Despite the efforts of management, however, resident abuse is getting worse. In the next section, I'll critique nursing home practices, with the belief that effective solutions aimed at reducing the incidence of resident abuse may be reached.

A Critique of Nursing Homes' Practices

There is a plethora of statistics on adult abuse in nursing homes. Whether or not they adequately explain the phenomenon of resident abuse is another matter. One certainty is that they have contributed to the growing conversation about resident abuse and (more importantly) establishing preventive measures for abuse. After reviewing existing research findings on abuse preventive strategies, the national center on elder abuse came out with the following in 2002:

- Assure *coordination* between law enforcement, regulatory offices, adult protection, and nursing home advocacy groups
- Support *education and training* to improve interpersonal caregiver skills with respect to managing difficult resident care situations, problem solving, and understanding cultural issues underpinning staff-resident relationships
- Improve *working conditions* in terms of adequate staffing, better communication between direct care and administrative staff, better pay, etc.
- Assure *compliance* with federal requirements concerning the hiring of abusive nurse aides
- Promote environments *conducive to good care*
- Assure strict *enforcement* of mandatory reporting and educate professionals and the public (non-mandatory reporters)
- Improve *support for nurse aides* (support groups)
- Support and strengthen *resident councils*
- Assure that *hiring practices* include screening prospective employees for criminal backgrounds, substance abuse, domestic violence, feelings about caring for the elderly,

reactions to abusive residents, work ethics, and ability to manage anger and stress

A look at the abuse preventive strategies above reveals a good understanding of the roles of regulators and nurses' aides. Together, they can create an environment in which residents will be cared for without mistreatment. Sadly (but not surprisingly), a great deal of nursing homes have continued (ignorantly or wickedly) to pursue practices directed at appeasing regulation and regulators. In doing so, managers of these nursing homes shy away from their managerial responsibility of effectively managing the nurses' aides—an important variable in the abuse-free equation. They (nursing home managers) are predisposed to implementing the pro-law type of abuse preventive strategies while almost completely neglecting the pro-nurses' aides strategies. My contention is not that law has no place in an operations environment such as a nursing home. Rather, I am calling for recognition of the contributory role played by core operations personnel, with respect to realizing the ideals that undergird those laws.

Again, going through what nursing homes do in terms of preventing resident abuse, continuous education and training of the primary caregivers (nurses and aides) appear most visible. This education and training (especially of nurses' aides) also double as the key abuse preventive strategy employed by the nursing home. As stated earlier, scenarios depicting varying forms of resident mistreatment are used to facilitate training. Though the scenario method of training can result in great learning outcomes, scenarios are often limited by the degree to which they replicate the desired state of learnedness. Training sessions in nursing homes are filled, for the most part, with scenarios that do not correctly represent the nursing home's operational climate. For instance, the following post-training quiz question on the vulnerable adult act (from the MRCI online training center) illustrates this point:

The failure or omission by a caregiver to supply a Vulnerable Adult with care or services including or not limited to food, clothing, shelter, healthcare, or supervision is neglect. True or False?

The answer, of course, is true. The wording is consistent with the vulnerable adult act's definition of neglect. It's worth noting, however, that the scenario either is silent on the ability of the caregiver to simultaneously attend to the needs of other residents (at that time), or possibly perceive of the care-giving environment as one just between the caregiver and the one resident in question. This perception of the care-giving environment is what frequently leads to cases of unwarranted punishment of core primary caregivers in the nursing home. An alternative look at the scenario, which is better consistent with the residents bill of rights (in my opinion), is one that speaks to management to provide (at every time) the necessary functional arrangement capable of adequately addressing the varying needs of all residents. If these arguments are insufficient to make the point, three scenarios (labeled A, B, and C) are presented and discussed next. The scenarios cover the areas of neglect, restraint, and physical abuse.

Scenario A

A resident who uses a wheelchair (and requires assistance during all transfers) needed to use the restroom. The resident had his call-light on and transferred himself from his wheelchair to the toilet after waiting for assistance but not receiving any for seventy minutes (as stated in the aide's termination of employment notice).

This scenario obviously indicates neglect, the degree of which (given the seventy-minute timeframe) speaks to the seriousness of the abuse. And if this were a case in a court of law, the ten-years-experience-fifteen-dollars-per-hour aide might need the combined expertise of Alan Baum and Tom Mesereau to save his CNA license. Fortunately for the nurses' aide, it was in a "court" presided over by the proverbial cock where every roach is pronounced guilty before coming in the presence of a judge. The aide was fired (still good enough that the former's CNA license was not revoked). Again, there is no intent to argue with the fact that the resident was abused. His request to use the restroom (within a reasonable timeframe) was denied—irrespective of whether it was intentional or not. Worse still, his transfer to the toilet was unsupervised. The resident was, therefore, exposed to a very high risk of falling . . . the result of which could have been fatal.

The question that seems reasonable is as follows: What managerial thinking and resources were put in place to accommodate, in a timely manner, the requests of not only the resident in the above scenario, but also the varying individual requests of all other residents? My knowledge of what happened on that fateful day reveals the following: all five aides on the schedule showed up for duty on that day, but due to ill-health, one had to go home almost at the start of the shift. Occasionally, replacement aides are called in, but there was no replacement for that shift. Though there was a trainee-aide on the floor, the aide could not have taken the place of the sick aide because all trainees have to be directly supervised for the duration of their training. This situation called for a split of the unit with the missing aide. This meant each of the four aides had to take two extra residents. As fate would have it, the resident in scenario A belonged to the unit with the missing aide, but he was voluntarily chosen as an extra by the aide who was fired in the same scenario. It is worthy of mention that two of the four aides regularly worked the short shift (3 p.m. to 9 p.m.), and one of these two was assigned the resident in scenario A. Generally, about 80 percent of the residents on the floor required assistance of two aides for one form of care or another. Present, also, were the two nurses on schedule. All four aides and two nurses were not strangers to the provisions of the residents' bill of rights and the vulnerable adult act.

True, the operational climate from which scenario A resulted may be subjected to a wide array of interpretations, but the inability of an aide to guarantee a timely response to the needs of ten aged, frail, and often alert residents cannot be easily dismissed. The reality of the nursing home setting is that, for every minute of an aide's time spent providing care for a resident, another resident is denied that time. With the existing aide to resident ratio, it is not uncommon for all the aides on a floor to be engaged with residents at the same time. Nursing home residents generally get impatient when in need (it is their right, and an aide does not need law school classes to know this). Ordinarily, nurses on the floor should help, but this depends on the facility's work culture. In facilities where effective teamwork forms an integral part of managements' styles and dispositions, residents' wait time may be reduced. To be fair to nurses who work in nursing homes, their daily routines are also demanding. In facilities where trained medication assistants (TMAs) are sparsely used, nurses get torn between passing out medication and dealing with an avalanche of documentation. Often, the volume of med distribution on a floor and during one shift will far outweigh biweekly sales by a local pharmacy in Twon Brass (where I was born). Nurses' help, with respect to residents' needs (those believed to be part of an aide's responsibilities) is therefore limited to the nurse's character. Some nurses may be favorably disposed to helping; others may not.

Going back to scenario A, how could the resident have waited unattended for seventy minutes when the resident's room was almost in front of the nurse's station? When the aide to whom the resident was assigned could be appraised by associates as hardworking, operations-savvy, quite helpful, fun to work with, and the very definition of a team player—the answer to the question may lie somewhere in the preceding paragraphs.

Scenario B

A male resident who suffered from dementia and frequent aggression (kicking, spitting, scratching, and cursing) had a towel wrapped (not tied) around his hands during a shower session.

In keeping with the well-known tradition in nursing homes, the two nurses' aides involved were immediately suspended and later fired by facility management. To discern the reason, I searched through my training notes and found the obvious answer. The towel wrapped around the resident's hands constituted placing a restraint on him, which only an MD could have authorized. Unauthorized placement of restraints amounts to physical abuse of the resident. Unlike in scenario A, it is extremely difficult to make sense of this decision. For instance, can one describe the act of wrapping a towel around a resident's hands as unreasonable if it was not intended to punish the resident and did not result in any injury? If we say the aides' conduct was not accidental or therapeutic, how would we describe the act of fastening the strap-on protective belt attached to bath chairs? Are these belts all MD-authorized?

To be sure, the care plan for the resident provided for the use of mittens (to be worn by the resident), long-sleeved gowns, and masks for aides during general care. Though regular mittens for the resident's in-room care were provided, the care plan was silent on how the resident's bath or shower was to be conducted (given the very combative behavior the resident). Waterproofed mittens for the resident's bath or shower were not provided. Although nursing home training sessions for aides convey—in a most unequivocal manner—the zero-tolerance position of the vulnerable adult act, the responsibilities of nurses' aides are often difficult to reconcile in the face of certain operational realities. Nurses' aides often don't know *how* to stay out of trouble. This is even truer with combative residents (and this will be discussed in detail in chapter three of this book). I advance the position that all resident behavior that is excessive or beyond normal must be thoroughly addressed by facility management. Training the aides, like they have always done, is not enough. Facility operations management personnel must craft doable ways of caring for difficult residents. The failure of facility management to do this leaves each aide on his or her own. The resident in scenario B, must have been given baths or showers by many aides at different times, but just how those services were conducted is anybody's guess. In the absence of a workable right way, some of them may have gotten away with comparable methods.

Scenario C

Resident C said to aide D, "You are rough."

"I want to go home" and "You are rough" might be the most frequently used sentences by residents of nursing homes. When residents say, "I want to go home," they may not be prompted by caregiver abuse. When residents say, "You are rough," however, suspicion of abuse arises. True, mere suspicion is not enough to warrant disciplinary action. The vulnerable adult act dictates that only physical evidence (in the form of skin bruises, redness, and swelling, for example) would be punishable. There have been cases, nevertheless, in which there is no real evidence of physical evidence, but aides have been charged with abusive conduct. In some of these cases aides have been punished by management for simply showing up for work. Management's may make such a decision if an accusation is repeated or an earlier (unconnected) accusation involves the same aide.

Three female aides were collectively accused of roughly handling a resident who needed three people to turn him.

One of the three aides was fired because she had been written up twice (not for related offences). In a meeting with facility management in which a male aide was informed of the decision to terminate his services after a case of neglect, he was shocked to hear that an earlier accusation of rough handling (which was investigated and dismissed) constituted one of the reasons for his termination. In both of these cases, the accusations were equivalent to evidence. There are other cases in which an aide may be repeatedly accused of doing something—even though he or she did not. For instance, the simple task of putting a pair of T.E.D. stockings on a resident is often construed as being rough. For aides who are assigned particular groups of residents to care for in weekly, biweekly, or monthly timeframes, the repetitive performance of this task ends up increasing the number of times they are likely to be accused.

The three scenarios discussed in this chapter in no way exemplify the entire spectrum of resident abuse in the nursing home. Cases of neglect—and the forms of physical abuse (including restraint—presented here seem to be daily occurrences. Aides' abusive conduct in terms of sexual, financial and extreme physical abuse seems more like a problem within general human society, not just nursing homes. Though they may rank lowest in the daily operational problems of nursing homes, they are very damaging when they find their way to the TV screen or newspaper. Nursing homes, in the eyes of the public, are seen as torture factories where nurses' aides, as torture masters, daily unleash their weaponry on society's aged, frail, and vulnerable population. Human society (outside of the nursing home) has continued to provide enormous resources to address the occurrence of such heinous acts. The nursing home—as part of that human society—will always be expected to play a collaborative role with the custodians of those resources.

What nursing homes have done—and are continuing to do—with respect to providing an abuse-free environment in which society's vulnerable adults are cared for—amounts to implementing the same strategies for heinous acts and those (though abusive) that are bound up with operations. For instance, if a male aide rapes a female resident in a nursing home, subsequent and far-reaching pre-employment background checks conducted on all potential employees may reduce such occurrences in the future. However, what will reduce the occurrence of the neglect seen in scenario A is not firing the aide. Rather, wait-time reduction strategies should be created, such as lowering the aides—residents ratio and establishing effective teamwork organizational culture. Again, though fellow aides and residents may not be adversely impacted by the arrest and detention of a rapist, the aide community (in the facility in which scenario A happened) is likely to lose motivation. Aides may embrace the work smart approach with care delivery. Like the popular saying goes, "When two elephants fight, the grass underneath them suffers"—the residents suffer from a drop in the quality of care they get (even if temporarily).

The foregoing is not a blatant suggestion that nursing assistants are always blameless when it comes to abuse that is operations laden. Sure, some aides are lazy, truant, and incompetent. Others may not be cut out for the job. In all of these cases, the point is that an organization that knows why it is in existence will (through its management) convey its destination to members and translate that destination into daily practices for members. The aides-are-the-problem foundation of management thinking indicates extreme managerial ineptitude. If aides are the problem, I do not see how the solution will come from the same aides? In response to her husband (who likes his meals to be rich in ingredients, despite the fact that he cannot support her financially), a woman from eastern Nigeria will say, "Sweet soup na money kill am." This is the woman's way of saying, 'I need money to purchase the necessary ingredients, with which, to prepare your delicious meal. Nursing home managers must learn, not only to talk, but *walk the talk*.

Final Words . . .

For all intents and purposes, the residents' bill of rights, the vulnerable adult act, and the elder justice protective acts were never conceived of as manuals of procedures (MOP) for the daily operations of management, staff, and residents of nursing homes. To the extent that they apply to nursing homes, they provide a picture of what the nursing home should look like—a favorable environment in which vulnerable adults will be cared for without any form of abuse. The responsibility of creating this environment—difficult as it is or may be—remains a major managerial function of nursing home management.

Presently, a combination of the physical environment of most nursing homes and the design of the core caregivers' (the CNAs) responsibilities create and perpetuate abuse. When a nursing assistant must (even while providing care to a resident) shuttle among eight to ten dependent residents, at least a couple residents will be denied timely care. To train nursing assistants that denial of timely care amounts to neglect (a form of resident abuse), and to teach them that care for residents must be provided in a manner that is not rushed is largely inadequate. A lesson on input/output relationships for nursing homes' management, may, be needed. The late afro-beat king, song writer, and social critic, Fela Anikulapo Kuti, once said, "Teacher no teach me nonsense."

Nursing assistants may be hired, fired, and even reported to the respective state department of health or the local police. One thing they all know is that, given the goal of getting a combative resident clothed, it will require far more than placing all known original documents of residents' rights and laws on the resident's bed. Finally, they will also agree that, if reading out these rights and laws is all management is to do to prevent resident abuse, then 5th graders can be called in to get the job done.

Chapter Three

DIFFICULT RESIDENTS AND DIFFICULT FAMILY MEMBERS

The responsibilities of nursing assistants in nursing home settings are not just enormous, but also challenging. For the nursing assistant, such challenges increase with either the promulgation of a new act or law dealing with elder care or heightening activities of elder rights advocacy groups. Both laws and elder rights activists tend to clamor for the rights of all elders in care-giving institutions. Accordingly, the same level of expectations for caregivers remains the same for all residents in facilities. However, just as a firm's level of output depends on the quality and quantity of its inputs (resources), effective care delivery services to nursing home residents depend on each facility's resources.

In the previous chapter, I made the argument that the level of management thinking, in a nursing home setting (with respect to effectively addressing legally defined expectations) is inadequate. Though that argument also runs through this chapter, I have refocused the discussion on difficult residents and difficult family members. I make the point that, in most nursing homes, management does not do a good job caring for difficult residents and managing difficult family members. To me, this leaves the majority of nursing assistants disgruntled, frustrated, and unmotivated. It is my belief that these feelings negatively impact quality of care.

I will start this discussion by providing definitions and characterizations of difficult residents and difficult family members—standpoints from which current nursing home practices will be looked at. As usual, I will determine the solidity of these practices as I try to take them apart in the way I know how. Finally, I present communication and collaboration as two powerful tools that management of nursing homes can use to address some of the friction created by difficult family members.

Who Is A Difficult Resident?

For the time I spent in the nursing home as a CNA, I witnessed with amusement the changes in nomenclature. They often referenced the same thing, but they sought to convey a higher status or level of dignity on a resident though, there was often no visible level of increase in status or dignity. Some of these changes in name are as follows: briefs, depends, dry prides, and undergarments. They all refer to the same incontinence product. Also, I witnessed the transition from bib to clothing protector, from nursing home to resident's home to neighborhood community. Briefs and bibs are befitting of infants or toddlers, and the names are therefore disrespectful when applied to elders. *Nursing home* suggests a confined environment, and it takes away from the desired dignity level of an adult. Those are the arguments put forth by proponents of these name changes.

It is not surprising, therefore, that residents' dignity scholars and advocates will find my *difficult residents* label offensive to adults who reside in a nursing home. To these thinkers, using the adjective *difficult* describes an elder's character and not the challenges that may result from the elder's physiological changes due to aging—something the elder does not have control over. I do not disagree with the notion of aging as the probable cause of physiological changes in an elderly person. I hold the position that, even for elders of the same age (and for those who suffer from the same ailment), the resultant physiological changes may be different. Some changes may produce challenges that require more of the caregiver's resources than others. My usage of the adjective *difficult* is intended only for classification purposes. Similarly, the following characterization of difficult resident draws from my observations (while working as a CNA) that these residents actually take more of the aide's time and energy than others.

Who, then, is a difficult resident? A difficult resident is that resident in a CNA's assigned group of 8-10 residents who requires either more of the aide's resources than most residents or keeps the aide disproportionately occupied. Generally, difficult residents share some of the following attributes:

- Those with ceaseless demands
- High-risk fallers, especially those that self-propel their wheelchairs and try to stand up at least once every five minutes
- Combative residents
- Those who require two or three aides for care at least three times per shift (with the exception of sleep time)
- Frequent bathroom users—including residents who want to use the bathroom three times per hour
- Those who perceive of the aide as their personal servant

- Those who possess massive and intimidating physiques (especially when non-ambulatory)

This list does not mean that a resident must neatly fit into all the categories to be seen as difficult. The true yardstick is the aide's resources (especially time and energy) needed by and given to a resident. Imagine a scenario in which an aide has three difficult residents in his or her assigned unit. There is a massively built and non-ambulatory resident in the tub room for his or her bath; the high-risk faller wandering in the hallway; and the third resident who ceaselessly yells, "help, help, help!" Does this look like a situation primed for abuse?

Difficult Family Members

Difficult family members are those relatives of residents (not limited to those with power of attorney) who look after their loved one by unbearably weighing on the emotional balance of an aide. Though facility management shares some of the heat from difficult family members, the aides, due to the frequency of their contact with residents, absorb the larger portion. For this reason, the aides' perception of difficult family members is that of a thorn in the flesh. If there is one thing an aide would wish for, it would be never having to deal with a difficult family member. Difficult family members create agonizing moments and they can cause the aide to lose his or her job. Interestingly, the aide would most likely choose a difficult resident over a difficult family member, and the facility management would more likely choose a difficult family member over an aide.

Difficult family members often have the following characteristics:

- Are highly picky in terms of the aide's conduct. Some family members lodge a complaint about an aide or a nurse during each visit.
- Often have a tall list of expectations from an aide with respect to their loved one.
- Often are self-centered, believing aides should do more for their family members.
- Sometimes, directly interfere with the aide's job by ordering aides around and acting like their supervisors.
- Always want to create jobs for aides even when not necessary. Some family members will indicate that their loved one wants to use the bathroom when that task is not actually required at the time.

- Display racist tendencies toward aides and nurses of different backgrounds.

Granted, some family members show legitimate concern for their loved ones. This list does not seek to cast aspersions on all difficult family members. Some of their actions may stem from their perceptions of how their loved ones should be treated, and they may be legally supported. My one concern here is how the behaviors in this list affect the aides' community in the nursing home. If the aides' community's group performance can be measured, is one likely to arrive at a higher performance level in settings with more difficult family members? Pending the outcome of such a study—and a reliance on my experience—I feel comfortable positing that difficult family members add to the frustration level of primary caregivers. As to whether or not these people will lead to plummeting performance levels that is up to management.

Nursing Homes in Action

This section takes a look at what nursing homes generally do to manage difficult residents and difficult family members. Though differences may exist among nursing homes in terms of what they do and the results they get, what is presented here seems to be common to most nursing homes. One instrument that is commonly used is the resident care plan. The care plan is a document that shows what is to be done for a resident, how it is to be done, and who is to get it done. A care plan exists for every resident. It is put together by facility management based on pre-admission (for new residents) information obtained from family members, existing medical records, and facility assessments. The care plan is expected to be regularly reviewed and updated with changes in a resident's condition. Even when not clearly delineated, a resident's care plan gives an indication as to the resident's behavior. For difficult residents, a suggested range of intervention techniques are listed. The resident care plan thus defines the basis for an aide's interaction with a resident—and all aides are expected to be aware of the contents of care plans whenever they provide care to residents. In summary, the resident care plan provides a tool with which facility management handles the challenges posed by a difficult resident.

Nursing homes also provide year-round in-service sessions and training for its employees. With reference to difficult residents, topics such as how to work with difficult residents, dementia, and customer service are discussed and often made mandatory. Sometimes, speakers from outside of a nursing home may be invited to facilitate a session. Other times, training sessions may be centrally organized with all nursing homes invited to participate. The sessions on dementia seek to inculcate in participants the need to *empathize* (not *sympathize*) with the resident. It goes through the concept of dementia as an umbrella name for a portfolio of diseases, the different stages of the diseases, and stage-appropriate behaviors and interventions. It concludes that the resident (suffering from dementia) has not chosen to be difficult. Instead, he or she has been conditioned by one or a combination of the diseases that make up dementia to so act. In "How to work with difficult residents" the sermon remains the same: "You cannot change the resident." The caregiver can only adjust his or her behavior to accommodate the unchangeable resident. Adopting the same underlying philosophical leaning as dementia training, customer service takes a high leap into the heavens and pronounces the resident king. The resident can do no wrong; all facility employees must be at the beck and call of residents. The idea is that all residents' requests must be promptly addressed to their satisfaction

As was mentioned in the previous chapter, in-house care conferences and floor meetings are avenues for the training of facility employees. Facility management utilizes such gatherings to review residents' behavior (with the expectation that improved ways of dealing with either a difficult resident or difficult family member will be discovered by the end of the sessions). The noticeable tradition with these meetings is for management to dwell more on an underlying possibility that aides may not be correctly following existing care-planned intervention techniques. (Hence the need for a refresher on the resident's care plans.) Like kindergarteners are taught to do recitation, aides are reminded to knock on a resident's door before entering, greet the resident, offer an introduction, stoop to the resident's eye level, maintain eye contact, speak slowly, tell the resident what you want to do, leave and come back if the resident refuses, and report to the nurse or supervisor if the resident still refuses. But when the resident does not refuse (and depending on the care to be provided), aides must work slowly, avoid rushing the resident, start conversation, talk about his wife or her husband, ask whether he or she likes mashed potatoes with gravy or Fufu with okra soup, ask him about his favorite sports team, etc. Most nurse managers and social workers believe this method is magical, a perfect formula that paves the way for smooth care delivery. Obsessing over this method, facility managers end up not giving needed attention to the nature and extent of the difficulty of the resident. When new ways of dealing with a difficult resident are reached, they either become operationally untenable or amount to mere "spray painting" of the old ways.

When it is believed that a given resident's behavior needs to—and can—be corrected through medication adjustment, facility management sets the ball rolling for the needed confluence of experts. The resident's physician or psychologist performs necessary diagnostic and prescriptive procedures. New medications may be prescribed for the resident, existing medications may be discontinued, and dosages may be altered to the direction of need. Aside from the highly experimental nature of this method (residents do not adjust to medications in the same manner), respective resident family members may not welcome the frequent alteration of their beloved's medications.

As far as what management of nursing homes do to manage difficult family members, I've never had the privilege of participating in any gathering of facility management and residents' families. It is, therefore, not known whether occasions provided by such meetings are used by management to address the problem of difficult family members. Judging from the filling-the-bed space preoccupation of nursing homes management and their disposition toward residents' family members in general, it is likely that management never recognizes the problem of difficult family members. And if management does recognize this problem, such family members are not supposed to be part of the solution.

Whatever the position of management is, regular complaints about family members by nurses' aides have only been met with solutions (from management) directed at the aide. These solutions seem to be: "Agreed that Mr. A. or Mrs. B. is difficult, it is your responsibility to work with him or her." Often, suggested solutions range from proactively doing everything Mr. A. or Mrs. B has asked the aide to do before he or she arrives at the facility to becoming a slave for Mr. A. or Mrs. B. For instance, a group of nurses' aides were advised by a ranking member of facility management to buy and present a birthday card to a family member (a person about whom the aides had just complained) on her next visit. The manager, though accepting the aides' complaint as worthy, proceeded to defend the family member because she was in a fragile mental state.

A Critique of Nursing Homes' Practices

The resident care plan could be an all-important document if it correctly estimated a given resident's behavior. It could direct the nurse's aide in terms of the what, how, and when of care. Perhaps the most important quality of a care plan is its timely reflection of the resident's condition. For instance, does a care plan for resident Y that is handed to aide Z describe resident Y as she is or as she was? Those who know the inner workings of nursing homes very well will confirm that there are two periods in every year when a resident's care plan can be fairly current. Those two periods are as follows: just prior to the department of health's annual survey and during the week of their exit. This is the period when facility managers run around like chickens with heads cut off. They fake best practices as far as workplace manners and relationships with aides.

There is another dimension to the residents' care plan, even when updated. The care plan is a manual of procedure with respect to providing certain specified care to a resident. Here and where possible, step-by-step procedures (to be undertaken by the aide) are detailed. A resident's care plan (or portions prepared in this format) often assumes the resident's behavior is static. That is, the resident must behave in the same manner in the absence of any observable change in condition. The relative permanence or sameness of intervention techniques—at least in the short term—may be seen from this perspective. Unfortunately, it is also this kind of assumption that renders the provision of care for a difficult resident extremely challenging (if not impossible). For instance, resident E, who is given to combative behaviors such as hitting and kicking, should be assisted by two aides according to the care plan. He seriously needed to have his undergarments changed.

To provide the needed undergarment change for resident E, aide F (the aide to whom resident E was assigned for the day) had requested the assistance of aide G. Aide G stood in front of resident E and explained to him what was to be done. Aide G loosely took resident E's hands in his two hands (as no aide is permitted to maintain a firm hold or grip on a resident) while aide F was behind resident E, cleaning out the mess. In one quick swoop, resident E grabbed aide G's left hand and bit one of his fingers. Aide G had to leave for the clinic. A scenario like this one exemplifies part of the challenging nature of an aide's job as he or she cares daily for difficult residents. A notable dimension of this difficulty is the fact that resident behavior cannot be timely predictive. And for most difficult residents, hitherto existing interventions will prove to be ineffective. This is the case with caring for residents with issues related to memory loss—and this situation reveals the breakdown of traditional care planning.

Social workers in nursing homes are always quick to tell aides about dementia and the unpredictability that often accompanies it. The same social workers will inform any in-house gathering of aides of the psycho-this-and-that of resident behavior. The aides know this, so management must do more than just knowing this. Has management demonstrated that it sounds any better than a scratched compact disc?

A floor meeting was called to address the challenging behavior of a resident. Present were three representatives from management, three nurses' aides, and a psychologist. As was expected, the meeting commenced with a review of the resident's care plan with emphasis placed upon determining the extent of the aides' compliance with the plan. Two of the aides in attendance (to whom the resident in question had been assigned) responded at length. They took time to point out the difficulty and frustration associated with working with the resident. One of the aides (a female) even narrated how the resident had kicked her in the stomach as she cared for him. The pain, according to the aide, was so intense that she had to scream out loud. At this point, one of the facility's managers advised the aide not to scream out in the future (even when kicked by the resident). The manager cited a research finding which claimed that noise aggravates residents who are given to combative behavior and agitation. After hearing this, another female aide responded that management did not know what it was like working with residents like the resident in question. The aide who was kicked had no choice but to leave the meeting in tears. The meeting ended without reaching a way forward but with management promising to do something. I suspect they have not done anything.

Nurses' aides in nursing homes have never pretended to be RNs, social workers, MDs, psychologists, behavioral scientists, or academic researchers. They know who they are—the ones who have to help get residents up in the morning, get them clothed, perform oral hygiene and grooming, assist with showers and baths, clean up all resident messes, help them get to the dining room, make sure they are fed, and answer their sundry calls all day until they go to bed. When they pretend not to know who they are, nurses' aides can always go back to those residents who collectively called them "poop cleaners." The truth, where it is corroborated, in the research which was cited by the manager, does not and will not put clothes on that resident, it will not change his undergarments, and it cannot stop the involuntary screaming resulting from being kicked by a stronger male. Even Jet Li may not have been able to absorb the lightning kicks of Bruce Lee without screaming.

On the customer service focus to solving the problem of difficult residents, the science remains that of effectively meeting the needs of the customer and not trying to change the customer in the short term. What the science is not, is that effectively meeting the needs of a customer (even the normal customer) is not some lip-service allocation of responsibility to a set of an organization's employees. Such employees must be able to either perform the needed service or be provided with what is needed for the desired level of performance to be actualized. A critical success determinant in the pursuit of customer-focused service entails making sure that the resources actually deployed are adequate to bring about the desired end state.

For instance, Resident J was assigned to aide K and asked aide K to put her on the toilet. Resident J can stand and ambulate with the assistance of an aide, but she cannot be left alone on the toilet. Resident J normally spends at least thirty minutes on the toilet. From there, she asks for the following: a glass of water, tissue paper on her wheelchair, a look at her Depends, the phone, etc. Finally, the resident is done and stands up to have her behind wiped. She repeatedly asks aide K to ensure that she is clean. She asks aide K to check whether the stool is sizeable, to tell the nurse to document it, to hand her the clean Depends, to pull her pants up, etc.

To say caring for resident J is challenging would be a gross understatement. An aide gets beaten down just by going through one toilet session. Resident J is only one of aide K's assigned residents, and the other residents often ask for aide K before he is done. The demands of others may be even more intense, leaving aide K panting as if being chased by a lion. As fast as aide K can run around, if he has to respect the pace set by his residents, he will find it an impossible task to meet the needs of his assigned residents. For alert residents whose needs aide K could not meet, aide K stands to be reported. Because resident J appears to be more likely to report than others, aide K will give more time to her. The point of this scenario is that, given the prevalent level of nursing homes' resource allocation, difficult residents make the realization of the ideals of effective customer service for all residents illusory. The aide is aware that he or she has to respond to all residents' call lights and requests, but whether or not the aide can respond in a timely manner will depend upon the number of requests, the nature of each request, and the time interval between requests.

The scenario with resident J illustrates some of the problems faced by caregivers in nursing homes. They are problems not only for the nurse's aide, but also for facility management. Whether by design or omission, participation levels of nursing home management in core care delivery is limited to decision making. This degree of participation is acceptable only if decisions are made properly. After all, it is commonly accepted that the effectiveness of a solution hinges on the extent to which the problem is factored in. Unfortunately, management continues to fail. A shift from this tradition may necessitate some of the following:

- Mandatory supervision of all core care services for very combative residents by designating a management representative. Such a representative must be hands-on and willing to make decisions on the spot. Like a field commander in a military operation, this person must be able to direct while participating in the activities of primary caregivers.
- Implementation of resident-centered care delivery culture—not the present lip service-oriented and deceitful arrangement. Dining, activities, and other services involving difficult residents must be rendered *as is* and not predetermined.
- The removal of non-core care services from the aide's responsibilities so the aide can be free to perform needed primary care delivery services. Volunteers can be used to answer call lights, monitor residents when they stand up, and perform all give-me-that services. The tradition of going from one floor to another to get needed supplies must be stopped.

- Admittance of residents who can actually be cared for given a facility's resources. This calls for an immediate abandoning of the current fill-the-bed-space drive. Potential residents must be thoroughly assessed for complexities.
- The strategic use of HR for recruiting and scheduling of employees. It makes no sense to employ and schedule an aide to work on a floor or unit where the aide will not be able to lift a resident's head or leg for the purpose of assisting the resident with clothing. Again, the pairing of nurses with aides on every floor must be anchored on the likelihood that the group can meet the desired goals. The idea that "an aide is an aide" or "a nurse is a nurse" must be abandoned.
- Realistic goals for all floor nurses and aides must be established.

Communicating and Collaborating with Difficult Family Members

What do family members of prospective nursing homes' clients know about nursing homes in general? What about the one which they have finally picked for their beloved? Generally, these family members—if they have lived in a society where nursing homes are prevalent—may have read about them, visited with friends, heard about them on news broadcasts, or talked about them with friends or relatives. Some may have even conducted online searches. When settling on a specific nursing home, they know what they have always known about nursing homes—plus what operatives of their chosen nursing home have told them. Does a family member's knowledge about nursing homes apply to his or her nursing home of choice? Put differently, does each nursing home (prior to the admission of any client) convey in exact terms the range of its service offerings and capabilities? Or do admission services coordinators of nursing homes act like commissioned salespersons who will stop at nothing just to get an empty bed filled?

I do not have a relative in a nursing home at the moment. I have not accompanied any prospective resident who is seeking admission. However, I have seen rooms, hardly big enough for a four year old and her collection of toys, advertised as spacious. I have seen these "spacious" rooms accommodating two vulnerable adults who are not related in any way. In my sojourn as a CNA, I have walked behind facility representatives as they conduct tours of the facility with family members of would-be residents. The one question I always asked myself during and after each parade session was, *Is this person talking about this facility where I work or some other place?*

My interest here is not whether this is salesmanship or marketing. And if it is marketing, I'm not interested in the arguments surrounding ethical or unethical marketing. Rather, I'm concerned about the results of these unwholesome image-laundering exercises. When nursing homes make promises they are not organizationally equipped to keep, management winds up empowering family members to respond in unpleasant ways. For instance, a difficult family member is more likely to react to the presence of a male aide at his mother's corner with the question, "What are you doing here?" if he was made to think that only female aides would provide cares for his mother. He is bound to become upset. True, he may decide to take his mother to another facility, if at the time of admission the facility could not guarantee his request for only female aides but that is still better for the latter facility than the alternative problems that may ensue. Legal action may follow after a breach in promise due to a huge disconnect between staffing of aides and floor requirements in nursing homes.

If the best any nursing home can do is to operate at a level of one aide for every ten residents, this should be disclosed to potential clients and their family members. Doing this is better than passing on the misleading information that aides respond to all call lights in five minutes (unless the facility can structurally support such a claim). Thus, effective communication is seen as conveying the array of services and resources of a nursing home to potential residents and their family members—especially before admission of the resident. Just as frontline officers of an organization should be versed in what their organization does and which departments or officers customers are to be referred to; nursing home admission coordinators should be knowledgeable about their organizations and honestly convey this to prospective clients. To do otherwise is to continue to create a gap between customer expectations and what the nursing home can offer. And because customer expectations in most nursing homes dwarf the organization's offerings, critical nursing home employees (such as aides and nurses) may be unduly exposed to the heat from difficult family members.

There must be some practical alliance between the nursing homes and family members in the provision of care to their residents. The present situation in which nursing homes update family members with the current status of their loved ones is not sufficient. For some difficult residents, either the presence of a family member or the provision of a particular care by the family member will make it easier for the resident. For instance, the act of shaving a resident who is combative can quickly lead to perceived abuse. I have seen how the spouse of a male resident handled this shaving task for a couple of years with success. Not only was she tenacious in terms of the regularity with which she visited, but she did a very thorough job of shaving him because he didn't resist her.

Most nursing home residents take their baths or showers once per week. Some difficult residents can go for two or three weeks without baths or showers because the aides cannot make them take one. Though it is easy to explain this away as an expression of their rights to refuse care, a problem arises when family members or facility management view this acts as insubordination on the part of the aides. An existing partnership of care delivery between the nursing home and residents' family members would resolve situations like this.

For the management of nursing homes, the preliminary task is to define the areas of needed cooperation, effectively communicate this reality to residents' family members, and get them on board the care-delivery train. Some family members voluntarily participate in care-delivery exercises, but their coverage is often limited to a handful of residents. Adopting collaboration as part of an all-inclusive management style by nursing homes' management would guarantee the provision of needed care to all manner of residents. Also, it would position residents' family members as participant observers—a position from which they could truly capture the challenges of caring for their loved ones. This experience may lead to narrowing existing gaps between themselves and caregivers.

Conclusion

Nursing homes' residents are not monolithic. They are different, and some of the differences among them place different demands on primary caregivers. Caring for some of them may require more of the primary caregiver's time and energy. Sometimes, meeting these strenuous demands leaves the caregiver with little time and energy to cater to other residents. If the primary caregiver is expected to uphold the same high standards while caring for all residents, then "something's gotta give." The primary caregiver must be freed from all non-core care giving activities. The core care services he or she provides must be defined in realistically doable terms, or they must be supervised by management. Furthermore, management must honestly communicate to families of residents what they (nursing homes) are equipped to do—and they must list the areas where family members can pitch in.

Chapter Four

Diversity Management: The African-Born CNA

Irrespective of size, most modern organizations claim to support diversity in their corporate mission or value statements. This is understandable given today's fast-changing global demographics. As cross-cultural migrations continue to tail growing economic activities, both societies and the organization become peopled with individuals from a wide array of backgrounds. Some organizations—especially the very large ones—have been compelled by anti-discrimination legislation *and* the potential rewards stemming from a culturally diverse staff. Others (mostly smaller and non-profit organizations) may have been recruiting culturally diverse employees just to satisfy legal requirements.

These different reasons for recruiting a diverse staff have varying effects. For instance, organizations that strategically utilize diversity not only end up satisfying legal requirements, but also allocate their resources in a way that will result in effective management of their diverse employees. Organizations in this group are more likely to consciously address the issue of workplace diversity than their counterparts whose appeal to diversity is largely intended toward fulfilling anti-discrimination laws. Organizations in the latter group need to begin programs directed at managing workplace diversity—and not because doing so make them more fashionable. Rather, they must begin these programs in order to retain the services of existing high-performing employees or effectively service their clientele (whose constitution may change very soon, if it is not already changing).

The nursing home is one organization where diversity management programs have to be stepped up. A Washington Post article (retrieved online) from August 26, 2009, stated that residents of all care facilities in the Washington area originated from 193 countries. The article noted that, "About 10 percent of people 65 and older in the United States are foreign-born." According to the same article, "The Pew Research Center estimates that by 2050, that figure will rise to 20 percent, with the total number of elderly immigrants quadrupling to about 16 million." For nursing homes in the United States, this calls for an intensification of efforts to service a culturally expanding market of residents and make sure its core primary caregivers stay motivated to providing needed services. Making sure that core primary caregivers stay motivated requires that management learn about the composition and cultural differences of this category of employees and promote the unique characteristics that define these individuals.

This chapter starts with a definition of diversity in an organization, and it narrows down to the nursing home environment. This will be followed by a discussion of the African Aide (NAR) with emphasis on the rationale for this choice. The chapter then moves on to what nursing homes have been doing to manage the unique differences of the African aide. And as usual, the chapter winds up with a critique of nursing homes' practices (including suggestions for improvement).

What Is Diversity?

Diversity, especially as it applies to a work environment, refers to the presence of various different types of people in an organization. These types may vary widely, depending on the size and composition of the organization, and they may include differences in education, race, ethnicity, skin color, physical attributes, gender, sexual orientation, job designations and positions, cultures, religious and political creeds, etc. Diversity in the work place rests on the notion that no one group or collection of groups of individuals (or their attributes and leanings) should enjoy elevated status to the detriment of others. The central idea of workplace diversity stretches far beyond the formal presence of various individuals with various characteristics. It encompasses the enactment of a workplace environment in which the potential beauty of individuality will result in the attainment of organizational goals. In this sense, workplace diversity in today's world is not just a happenstance. Instead, it's a reflection of global population dynamics—the need for an organization to look into various demographics in order to thrive.

Consistent with the concept of diversity is the insufficiency of cultural plurality—by itself—to deliver an organization's expectations. According to Thomas, Jr (2012), "This is no longer simply a question of common decency, it is a question of business survival." The business survival of any organization—be it a large corporation or a non-profit charitable organization—is the critical responsibility of its management. It is the place of management to consciously channel the disparate traits and creeds of its diverse employees in a way that will produce expected results. Diversity, on its own, may be useless and counterproductive if not directed by the needs of an organization and skillfully "midwifed" by its management. The point is, diversity cannot be talked about or perceived in ways that isolate what an organization's management does to secure its culturally heterogeneous work force.

What, then, should be the guiding principle or philosophical tenet of diversity management? Thomas, Jr (2012) provided an answer in a question posed to all those who manage diverse employees. The question is, "Am I fully tapping the potential capacities of everyone in my department?" Scenarios where some employees (identical in traits and creed) withhold or are ill-empowered to produce to their potential capacities are indicative of shortcomings in existing diversity management efforts or the lack thereof. Hence there is a need for strategic rethinking.

In a sense, diversity management is analogous to employee motivation efforts in an organization. The fundamental difference is that most organizations standardize motivation efforts and programs. Diversity management does not aim to "uniculturize" all the employees of an organization. Instead, such management accepts extant employee multiculturalism and solicits and secures optimal performance from each employee. In conclusion, therefore, the concept of workplace diversity expresses the 21st century confluence of individuals with a wide array of differences. In a work environment, however, the objective is for managers to seek ways of making the work environment a haven for heightened individual productivity (without necessarily creating advantages for certain employees).

The African-Born CNA

Other than statistics that broadly classify African aides as black workers, numerical specifics on the presence of African-born African aides in nursing homes do not seem to exist. Going by a 2006 estimate, the black population of nursing home aides made up 35 percent of all nursing home direct care employees in the United States. The white population (with 51 percent) is the most prevalent (Smith & Baughman, 2007). The same estimate puts the figure for all foreign-born aides in nursing homes at 17 percent. Arriving at the percentage of African-born African nursing assistants in the United States would require extracting all people not born in Africa from the 17 percent figure. Whatever is left becomes the estimate for the African-born African nursing assistant population in nursing homes. So what? Just hold your breath for a minute, and I'll advise.

Generally, in nursing homes with a fairly high degree of interracial employees, a job-type distribution of employees would reveal a high concentration of whites in all positions but the nursing assistant role. At any point in time, a greater percentage of members of other races fill in vacancies for nursing assistants. When further reduced to just members of all other races (with the exception of whites), African-born people become the ones to beat. The African-born African nursing assistant can be considered the nerve center of the primary care delivery unit of most nursing homes in the United States. They are always present, always dependable, and always willing to work (even when ill). They take the fewest vacations, and they are the most mistreated. Like a fly attracted to a piece of rotten meat, they stay glued to the nursing home. They breathe, eat, think, and live the nursing home. Their understanding of the spirit of competition that undergirds America's greatness is that of scrambling for open shifts. They become "double machines" as they pick up or hop from one nursing home to another to work double shifts.

In so many respects, the nursing home is home to many African-born Africans in the United States. Though a good number of those who are currently in other occupational categories paid their dues at one time or another before moving on, the picture looks different today. Job projections favor the health sector, and the harsh competitiveness of placements in the other sectors appears to be attracting and retaining more African-born Africans (either as nursing assistants or nurses) than it is losing to other sectors. It is not uncommon to hear an African nursing assistant say, "I am better than an engineer or a lawyer," "As long as I am strong and hardworking, I can pick hours and make more money than them." For a whole lot of others outside the health sector (who have gone through or are going through) the harrowing experience of frequent layoffs, their song is, "If I knew when I came to America what I know today, I would have studied to become a nurse instead of . . ." Given the relative homogeneity and group-think character of most African cultures, the resultant bandwagon effect from such statements could be likened to a million-man match in support of a course.

It is clear that the African-born nursing assistant (and in some respects, the African community in the United States) is wholeheartedly committed to the business of nursing homes. It is also apparent that the level of commitment is such that the African-born nursing assistant does more to solve the staffing problems of the nursing home than the latter's management. As dependable and readily available people (a level that may be second only to the military),

African-born nursing assistants—often with a very low call-in record—frequently pick up the slack when others can't work. In spite of the presence and importance of the African-born nursing assistant, he or she is more likely to end up as the proverbial baby to be thrown out with the bath water. He or she is the one who is emotionally abused by residents, family members, and management—and the one who is made a stranger in his or her home.

I feel comfortable—despite the risk of being accused of trumping the race card—asserting that the bulk of the mistreatment meted out to the African-born nursing assistant derives from the diversity-averse disposition of the nursing home work environment. It is my thinking that strategically recreating the nursing home work environment (with the aim of promoting true diversity beyond the mere recruitment of culturally different people) is valuable. It will not only preserve the loyalty and commitment of the African-born nursing assistant, it will also motivate them to perform better. In the next section, I will examine the practice of diversity management in nursing homes.

Nursing Homes in Action

Many diversity management experts will come to the conclusion that most organizations are yet to thoroughly come to grips with what diversity management truly involves. Most organizations have not benefited from their efforts at managing diversity. This is in spite of the Society for Human Resources Management's (SHRM) 2006 observation that, "Seventy-six percent of organizations have practices in place that address workplace diversity." Before jumping to the conclusion that such practices are ineffective, it is best to identify and understand some of them. Here, I am talking about the practices nursing homes engage in to manage workplace diversity. Again, I recognize the possibility of inter-nursing home differences. What follows is a list of some of the practices nursing homes engage in to manage diversity.

Hiring and Recruitment: If there is one thing certain about the hiring and recruitment practices of most nursing homes, it is that their employees come from a diverse multicultural background. Nursing home employees are of different races because they are from different countries. They occupy different positions—among them are homosexuals, transsexuals, heterosexuals, Christians, Muslims, Hindus,

Democrats, Republicans, independents, nurses, nursing assistants, dietary aides, maintenance personnel, social workers, supervisors, managers, directors, etc. The hiring and recruitment practices of nursing homes are based on their status as equal opportunity employers (EOE), conditioned by existing laws to pursue anti-discriminatory policies.

Education and Training: After recruitment, nursing home employees must attend required orientation programs designed to socialize them into their new organization. Diversity is an area of emphasis during new employee orientation sessions and subsequent year-round training sessions. Often, the HR personnel in charge draw the attention of employees to the facility's mission and value statements with respect to diversity. They stress the facility's status as an equal opportunity employer and tell staff members to uphold non-discriminatory behavior. Employees are charged with respecting the wide array of their individual differences as they work together. Sometimes, instances of previous inappropriate behavior and sanctions earned are cited to drive home the facility's zero-tolerance posture on matters of this nature.

Celebration of Cultural Day: It is also the practice of some nursing homes to set a day for the celebration of employee cultural heritage. Usually directed and overseen by members of a facility's activity department, nursing home employees are asked to turn up in attire that showcases their cultural heritage. In the gathering of fellow employees, management, and residents, participating staff members display their cultural attire. They say what the attire is called and explain its origin. Depending on a facility's diversity and the turn out, such days can be very colorful.

A Critique of Nursing Home Practices

The closest resemblance of diversity and diversity management (within the context of managerial practices in nursing homes) occurs when workers are recruited and hired. A lot of nursing homes in the United States employ a competitive number of workers not born in the United States. This perpetuates the impression that they (the nursing homes) are living up to their avowed pro-diversity claims. Of course, an American-based organization can show that a sizeable proportion of its employees are foreign-born and thus seem culturally diverse—albeit superficially. However, diversity management is not just a numbers game. There is—and must be—a qualitative dimension to it.

In a master's degree thesis on race, power, and workforce diversity submitted to the department of psychology at the University of Alabama in 2011, it was observed that, "The status of today's nursing home is characterized by racial inequalities in the distribution of staff across the tiers of power and leadership" (Vinson 2011). The researcher further observed that, though workplace diversity in nursing homes could be readily seen at the direct care level, the composition of administrative and leadership positions is uniculturally skewed. Again, a nursing home with dissimilar circumstances may exist, but my experience is consistent with Vinson's. In the case of two nursing homes well known to me, positions such as administrator/CEO, director of nursing, HR management, business office manager, sales and marketing, director of social work, head of activities/therapy, head of maintenance, and head of dietary services are filled by white Americans. In most cases, all line staff positions in these departments are occupied by white Americans (though there are some exceptions in dietary services and laundry). African-born Africans function as nurses (mainly LPNs) and certified nursing assistants (CNAs)—but more often the latter.

Because my focus is on how the African-born certified nursing assistant has been managed by nursing home leadership, I'd like to explore Vinson's argument further. The race-exclusionist leaning of nursing home leadership partly translates into an avalanche of discriminatory practices against African-born CNAs. First, the issue of discrimination against Africans in a nursing home setting is not in doubt. Vinson's research drew from earlier research to buttress the fact that discriminatory practices against minorities were taking place. The study showed that, "Well over 70 percent of CNAs experience blatant racism on the job" (Vinson 2011). For the African-born African CNA, "blatant racism" is experienced every day and during every shift. I will briefly discuss the manifestation of racist practices using three scenarios.

Scenario A:

An African-born African CNA is perceived by some as a horrible communicator who speaks with an accent.

To all foreign-born who reside in the United States, the social stigma of not understanding English due to their inability to speak in a recognizable American accent—is one that is dealt with quietly on a daily basis. The tradition seems to be one of docile acceptance on the part of the foreign-born, something about which nothing can be done. It is a disability with which the foreign-born must live. The larger society may continue to perpetuate this stigmatization of the foreign-born, but when an organization (especially one that claims to promote diversity) ends up accepting and acting out this behavior, its diversity claims should be dumped in the trash.

A nursing home handpicked some African-born African CNAs for the purpose of teaching them to speak like Americans. A white American was contracted to facilitate the learning sessions, and the CNAs were advised not to discuss the meeting with anyone outside of the class. The sessions commenced and ended with the CNAs unable to speak like Americans. True, this may look like a case for an ACLU lawyer, but that is not the point here. My concern is not the underlying assumption that ineffective communication may negatively affect care-delivery services in the nursing home. I am perturbed by the fact that these CNAs were interviewed and hired by a white American. Worthy of mention, also, is the fact that none of the pre-hire interview sessions was conducted in the CNAs' native language. At the time of this ill-fated American-English class, these CNAs had worked in the facility for not fewer than two years. They demonstrated a solid understanding of their residents and their job responsibilities. What, then, was management's rationale for this American-English training?

The nursing home, like any other gathering of Americans and Africans, is another venue for the stereotypical American to complain about anything that is not American. These Americans will never understand Africans because, from their standpoint, the African should speak like them. If one does not speak like them, one has an accent. And the cure for this is obviously to eliminate the African's accent. Is there something like good logic but poor reasoning? Somebody, help me out here. Again, these Americans (as their resumes will likely read) are supposed to be excellent communicators, but communication does not include listening for them. Ayebaifie, my seven-year-old, was born and raised in Minnesota. He always says, "Daddy, your English is weird. You speak like an African." Yet, Ayebaifie understands this "weird English" of mine. I guess *he* is the excellent communicator.

With respect to diversity and its management, the action of "training" the African-born CNAs to speak like Americans is completely wrong. Anchored in arrogance-informed ethnocentrism, it runs counter and defeats the aim of effectively managing workplace diversity. It creates a work environment in which some people are declared to be superior to others. The skill set and knowledge base of speech and language therapists, communication experts, and American-English teachers is not useless in any way. In the nursing home, given the immense contribution of the African-born African CNA, this repertoire of communication skills can be better used to redirect the stereotypical American toward an enhanced understanding of the African-born African CNA. White Americans, after all, do not all speak in the same accent, and it is not known whether the same facility has had a similar training program to standardize their accents. Similarly, errors in grammar and spelling in documents authored by white Americans and posted on official notice boards are daily occurrences. If the stereotypical white American can read and understand such documents, he or she can attentively listen to and understand the African-born African CNA as the latter communicates in the most general form of the English language.

Scenario B:

There is disparate treatment of African-born African CNAs vis-à-vis their white American-born counterparts.

I do not intend to continue the rather philosophical debate on the extent to which objective reality—even in a nursing home—is or is not possible. By the same token, I'm not about to insinuate that the policy thrust and actions of nursing home managers are race-driven. If anything, I have a problem with the negative impact some nursing home managers have on African-born African CNAs. Typically, the African-born African CNA is of the opinion that he or she is not treated as well as the American-born aide. It is widely believed that this unfavorable treatment manifests in areas such as assignment or allocation of residents (where African-born African aides are more likely to be assigned more difficult residents); management's selective handling of complaints from aides (complaints from white aides receive more attention and condition management's response); the granting of permission to stay off-duty or enjoy a leave of absence; the demeanor or body language of management personnel when they address the African-born African aides; the level of workplace socialization between key members of management and a select group of aides (who are mostly American-born); and the differences in punishment between aides from both races for similar offences.

I accept the possible role of race-colored perception in these beliefs. In a society in which a set of people have suffered deprivation and varying forms of race-laden oppression for a long period of time—and in which members of the dominant race still occupy the top echelon of management—little can be done to correct views held by members of the other group. The p.m.-crew of nursing assistants had just started their shift when a resident complained of discomfort while seated in a wheelchair. A couple of aides tried repositioning the resident. Soon after, the resident was almost sobbing, and the aides decided to put the resident in bed. To the surprise of the three aides, the resident had a bedpan tucked in his depends, and he had been seated on that in the wheelchair for an indeterminate amount of time. It was generally seen as an anomaly to be accounted for by the a.m. crew (given the timing of the discovery). The incident was reported to the appropriate authority. Whatever management looked for or at in the course of their investigation is not known, but the aide whom the resident was assigned to in the a.m. shift remained untouched. To the in-facility African-born African aides, an offence of this nature could have led to immediate dismissal if it was connected with any one of them. People in that marginalized group can list a number of African-born African aides who either got fired or were asked to resign for lesser offences.

In another nursing home, an American-born white aide was removed from the floor (though temporarily, and obviously not due to poor health) to function as an assistant in the activities department. The same feeling of race-induced choice went through the minds of the African-born African aides who worked on that floor. To them, this was a lighter job than that of a nursing assistant, and so it was given to *their* person. Again, management may have its reasons for this action, but that an ad for the position never existed, coupled with the lack of pre-known criteria, for this choice, fueled the perception (if it was) of the African-born African aides. Both examples point to the nursing home reality: a workplace peopled by race-diverse human beings who are not treated equally. Maybe nursing home managers have to listen, and re-listen to late Bob Marley's *War* (substituting racial tension for war).

Scenario C: There is a contemptuous disregard for African culture.

There are aspects of African culture—even in modern times—which should be respected by whomever the African come in contact with. Doing so is not doing a favor to the African; neither is the African pleading for the recognition of others. Rather, respecting certain pieces of culture is akin to showing respect for another human being. Two of these aspects—though not confined to the nursing home work environment—are African names and African food types. In the nursing home (as in most other work environments in the United States), there is a tangible degree of disdain or rejection of African names and food types. Based on my observation, white Americans are more likely to be disrespectful than others. Despite the fact that most African names today are spelled in English letters and free of diacritical marks, white Americans have never shown interest in pronouncing these names correctly (especially fairly long names). Sometimes, these people may have worked with the same African person for a long period of time. In this case, the African often accept an abridged form of his or her name under the guise that it is the normal thing to do. The problem is not just the loss of the historic event or situation (upon which most African names are founded), but also the fact that, subsumed under the façade of normalcy, there is an entrenchment of the superiority of one lifestyle over another. This is a serious concern for diversity management.

The African-born African worker in most organizations in the United States enjoys the same legal entitlements as workers from other races to bring in food of his or her choice. For some African-born African employees, the pursuit of this simple legal entitlement has proven to be a source of discomfort—one caused by the intolerance of a coworker who is often from a different cultural background. There have been several cases in which African-born African employees were told that their foods were stinky. To be fair to management, whenever such cases are reported, the culprits are seriously cautioned. Still this is only a victory for the African-born who is psychologically strong enough to withstand the emotionally discomforting experience. For the many others who adopt the after-all-this-is-their-country mentality (beaten into cowardice by other forms of blatant racism), the only option is to stop bringing that type of food to work. The nostrils of other culturally divergent coworkers become the litmus test for whether a certain type of food may be brought to work.

I bring up these issues to stress the diversity-management needs of nursing homes where African-born African workers play an important role. I do not mean to paint nursing homes as centers of blatant racism. It is not known whether the mainly white management of nursing homes is different culturally from management in other organizations within the United States. Sociologically speaking, the tendency to act out in ways culturally predetermined does not constitute an offense by itself. But it would be inimical to society if such acting out no longer brought about its advancement. The advancement needs of society and its organizations require that existing culturally predetermined ways of acting out be continually updated.

Effectively managing diversity, in the nursing home with a huge presence of African-born Africans would at least require a functional representation of this community at all tiers of power and job classifications. The author must acknowledge, however, that mere representation may not necessarily deliver the desired results. There are ample instances where an African-born African CNA would become a nurse and either get powerlessly sucked-up into higher management, or naively view his/her new position as success from hard work (of course) and upon which to assume that whatever mistreatment an African-born CNA suffered was inextricably tied to the latter's job status. In this sense the African-born African CNA is advised to aspire to either become an LPN or an RN.

On another front, because power relations in organizations are hardly different from what one sees in the organization's larger external environment, it is doubtful that even an overwhelmingly lopsided composition of management by African-born Africans at the nursing home level would effect a significant change without corporate-level support. It is in recognition of this—and the previous discussion—that I recommend the following steps (not necessarily in the order listed). They will assist with the management of diversity as it pertains to African-born African CNAs in the nursing home.

- Incorporate diversity into the organization's strategy at the corporate level. This should differ significantly from the traditional practice of merely stating in its mission statement that the organization promotes diversity. A diversity-promoting management unit should be created via HR at the corporate level. Corporate-level executives are usually U.S.-born—this unit should be headed by a qualified foreign-born.
- Ensure that the composition of management at the nursing home level is moderately representative of its diverse staff. Specifically, the facility administrator, director of nursing, and HR manager must not be members of the same race.
- Create a facility-level monitoring unit that will only report to the diversity-promoting management unit at corporate.
- Establish a pre-hire attitude test for all potential employees. Simply stating that one possesses excellent communication and interpersonal skills does not mean anything. At the end of the day, this may boost the competitiveness of the stereotypical white American in a fast-changing and increasingly competitive world.
- In nursing homes with an appreciable presence of the African-born CNA, the yearly 4-6 weeks' vacation period needed for them to visit their birth countries

should be accommodated by respective facility policies. Nursing homes can create vacation calendars and minimum service-periods for the CNAs to forestall shortfall in staffing due to longer absences. The practice (upheld by some nursing homes) in which an African who intends to undertake a trip(especially when he/she has enough accumulated paid-time-off hours to cover the trip) is required either to source his or her replacement or resign is needlessly punitive.

- All facility-sponsored potlucks and cookouts should adequately reflect the cultural diversity of its employees. Nursing homes should emulate the practice by an Illinois-based facility where meals of staff members' home countries are occasionally served. There is nothing wrong with making this practice a regular one. As for which African meal to serve, the yardstick should be the concentration of Africans from different countries in the facility. Generally, the nursing home is peopled by Africans from Ghana, Liberia, Nigeria, Cameroon, Sierra Leone, Senegal, Kenya, Uganda, Togo, Somalia, Ethiopia, and Sudan. A combination of Liberian jolof-rice or rice with cassava leaf, Nigerian rice and stew, or fufu and okra soup, Ghanaian kenke, Kenyan ughali, and Ugandan samosa in a rotational manner will work perfectly fine.

The facility's designated dietary personnel should get the recipes from individual staff members from these countries.

- Nursing homes with many African-born CNAs should display—in all open areas—posters with pictures of a cross-section of its diverse employees. The posters should bear the following inscription: "This facility is diversity friendly." Accordingly, all potential residents and their family members must be properly informed (prior to admission) of the facility's culturally divergent employee composition. Where consistent with other resident rights and state and federal laws, family members and residents can consent by signing a prepared form.

Because nursing homes differ in size, policies, and resident and staff composition, the steps I have listed are only guidelines for sustainable and improved performance. Facilities, depending on their resources, can add to this list. The one important thing is that nursing homes that fit my lengthy discussion (in this chapter) cannot continue to exist in the same way they have always existed. Something must be done!

Conclusion

Diversity management in a workplace is not synonymous with the simple hiring of people of different creeds and cultural backgrounds. It is more of the challenging task to retain these differences in an organization's workforce while wringing out the best performance from everyone. A very fundamental and integral aspect of diversity management lies in creating a workplace where no one set of people or values reign supreme. The various people who make up an organization's workforce must also be represented in all job categories. Obviously, this is an arduous responsibility for management, and that is why it must be a component of an organization's strategy at the corporate level.

In a nursing home setting where African-born African CNAs tirelessly and productively function to translate the dreams behind primary care delivery for society's elderly into reality, management must act. The least management can do is psychologically tune itself and every other member of the nursing home community into accepting the unique differences of the African-born CNA. To do otherwise is to treat the African-born African CNA as if he or she (despite his or her thankless and immeasurable contribution) is some "recipient of generosity" (Thomas, Jr 2012) of a dominant white culture. This has been the bane—and will continue to be the bane—unless something is changed in terms of diversity management in most organizations within the United States.

Chapter Five

A Model for Nursing Home Management

"It's Time to Make Management a True Profession" (Khurana & Nohria 2008) is the title of an essay authored by the two renowned Harvard Business School professors of business administration. Published in the October, 2008, edition of the Harvard Business Review, the article focused on the loss of legitimacy of managers due to growing public distrust for them. The authors attributed this development to the failure of private businesses to self-regulate—hence the need for a return to the original credos behind the conception of formal management education and the role of the manager. The authors agreed that lost public trust in managers can be regained if the practice of management is made a true profession (replete with a set of codes and standards for ethical conduct that managers must conform to). Of particular interest to me—especially with regard to the title of this chapter—are two requirements for the practice of management. The first is the moral dimension of managerial practice, and the second is the knowledge or education component of the manager.

Starting with the second of the two requirements, it is commonly accepted that the manager of any organization should possess some knowledge relevant not only to the successful performance of his or her duties, but also to the attainment of the objectives of the organization. The problem lies in what constitutes relevant knowledge. Generally, most nursing homes are headed by administrators who have gone through the required state certification and licensure process. But as most employees of nursing homes will agree, the Director of Nursing (DON) is the commander in chief. Whereas the administrator concentrates more on budgetary compliance and external relations issues, the DON (obviously a licensed nurse who may possess a degree in nursing) asserts authority on the length and width of primary care delivery activities. The DON is responsible for the hiring and firing of floor supervisors, nurses, and CNAs; the assignment of CNAs to residents, the decisions on quality of care, for example.

Broadly classified, the sphere of the DON's authority covers both core nursing and managerial activities. The DON—by training and certification—possesses relevant knowledge to function in a range of core nursing capabilities. But many DONs who have spent three to five years in their current status can hardly function as nurses—even in a nursing home setting. This results from the fact that they believe they are managers. Such DONs will prefer immediate retirement to translating and transferring their relevant core nursing knowledge to a core nursing role in today's hospital environment. This is because they have probably forgotten some of what they were taught while training as nurses. They have not updated their skill set in ages. Are they doing better as managers of nursing homes than they could have done as trained nurses? Obviously, one cannot say. However, I can reply with an uppercased *NO* when asked whether or not DONs possess adequate relevant knowledge to perform the range of managerial functions they have either been given or ascribed to themselves.

As far as the moral dimension of managerial practice goes, my guide remains the extent to which such practices could be seen as fair to both the nursing home resident and the CNA who cares for the former. I further look at fairness from the likelihood that a set of managerial activities—with respect to primary care delivery—will result in the attainment of resident satisfaction if measured by their ADL needs. Again, and without starting a debate on the superiority of the our-customers-come-first approach or the our-employees-come-first approach to achieving organizational goals, it suffices to say that both approaches can lead to the same desired result. For instance, a nursing home that has always sung the our-customers-come-first song had two CNAs on the floor during a state department of health survey. This was not just that there should have been three aides (going by the 1:8 formula), but that one of the two CNAs barely knew where to get what on the floor, talk more of knowing the residents. This is because the stranger CNA had barely worked on that floor, and had to depend on the regular CNA for directions. It was like twenty-four residents being taken care of by one CNA and a trainee

Can one say that the actions of management—as far as staffing that floor on that day—were fair to the residents they claimed occupied a top position in their list of priorities? Obviously, management was not fair to the two CNAs either. So what happened to primary care delivery? Successfully completed, or neglectfully and abusively accomplished? A true implementation of the client-first approach through customer satisfaction would have required the timely provision of needed care for the residents at all times. Some nursing homes adopt a make-believe approach during health department surveys by flooding the floor with all categories of employees and making them available to the residents and CNAs. CNAs are temporarily treated as kings because there are often more hands to help than needed.

Due to the temporary nature of such practices, the hypocrisy that undergirds them, and the wavering commitment of nursing home managers toward residents' needed care, it's not hard to make some claims. For example, the case can be made for a required minimal level of commitment to residents' well-being as a mandatory requirement for nursing home management. Similar to the code of ethics advocated for managers by Khurana and Nohria, an integral part of the code of ethics for nursing home management should spell out a better and more realistic aide-to-resident ratio, for instance. In my view, such a ratio should be 1:4 for every 8-hour shift.

I'd like to move to the most challenging part of this book: providing recommendations on how nursing homes should be managed. To many, criticism is cheap. What is novel is coming up with effective solutions. Often, the tendency is to pick apart the recommended solutions offered by a critic, especially by card-carrying members of the other group. This is done in a bid to maintain the status quo. Fortunately, this book is not about the world's hunger problem (to use a line from one of my lecturers), and I did not promise to have that solution. Rather, this book is on aspects of nursing home management—aspects that have a direct bearing on primary care delivery. Specifically this book focuses on how CNAs assist residents—who, due to the aging process, have become weak and almost totally dependent—with ADLs. The design of the CNA's job, the resources provided for the former to work with, management's thinking with respect to the CNA's job, the residents and their independently determined individual needs/requests—these all combine to define what happens on the floors of nursing homes. The scenarios used to describe the nursing home, in this book, were all real-life experiences from the floors of existing nursing homes that occurred when the author worked as a CNA. It is from the authenticity of these scenarios (as supporting pillars of the discussions and descriptions held so far) that I present a model for nursing home management. The model will be better understood by describing the component parts.

The Model

This model rests on the assumption that corporate bodies of nursing homes are committed to the business (irrespective of whether they are for-profit) of providing needed care for the aged population of society. It is necessary that this commitment is demonstrated in the provision of necessary physical structures (such as buildings and spacious rooms with reasonable amenities). With this in mind, the model runs as follows:

Composition and Structure of Facility Management: Presently, management at the nursing home level is made up of a licensed administrator (an assistant administrator in some cases), the director of nursing, a human resources manager, and the various heads of department (such as maintenance, director of social work, therapy, and dietary services). Though I do not find this composition troublesome, I suggest the following modifications:

- In addition to states' licensure requirements, the facility administrator must possess formal training in management. A bachelor's degree in either management or business administration should be the minimum. A bachelor's degree in healthcare management would also suffice.
- The administrator must be able to demonstrate understanding before corporate level panelists at the time of interview. He or she must indicate knowledge of the managerial dynamics of a modern organization.

He or she must demonstrate ability to benchmark best practices outside of core nursing home businesses and effectively translate the same to success strategies for the nursing home.

- The administrator must function as the CEO of the facility and either define the facility's direction or effectively locally anchor one prescribed by corporate. Whatever the case, he or she must ensure consistency of all facility practices with stated directions. The ability to establish landmarks to gauge facility practices is vital here.
- A facility administrator must possess excellent people skills and other soft skills necessary for today's work environment. He or she must strike a balance between the numerous demands of residents and employee motivational needs. The right candidate is not the one who ends up sermonizing. The right candidate knows that it takes a manager—not the law—to move an organization from one level to another.
- Consistent with the other points, the classic and presently all-powerful DON (professionally trained as a nurse) should be stripped of facility manager responsibilities. Retaining the same title and place as a member of facility management, the director of nursing should be the head of facility core nursing activities.

He or she should have the primary responsibility of supervising all facility nurses to ensure that in-house nursing practices conform to standards established by appropriate professional bodies. This candidate, in addition to being an RN, must have functioned well as a floor nurse and still possess the passion for floor nursing. For instance, in an emergency situation with a bleeding resident, this candidate should feel professionally comfortable taking the lead to stop the bleeding.

- Another RN of the same professional status with the director of nursing (but with a flair for practical care delivery) should be appointed a chief operations officer. Saddled with the responsibility of training facility employees, this person must be floor-oriented, hands-on, and in possession of the acumen to translate broadly defined care delivery standards into concrete and doable practices for certified nursing assistants. This person must also be able to regularly demonstrate—through active participation—how to provide ADLs to difficult and combative residents. Care delivery operations happen on the floors (and often *as is*), so this officer should demonstrate the required skillset on the floors and with real residents exhibiting real behaviors.

- Finally, all floor managers must—to a large extent—be operations savvy or favorably disposed to that modality. A trained nurse who cannot single-handedly effect the transfer (using a gait belt of a resident who is an assist of one) from the resident's bed to a wheelchair has no business being on the floor in the first place. To put it mildly, this would be like having four people in a car on a road trip from Saint Paul to Chicago with all of them but the driver certified to drive a motor vehicle. With the same luck, a blind man could drive to Chicago. If, however, the need for experimenting arises, an officer who can hardly distinguish between a .45 automatic and an AK47 should be made to command the combat-ready U.S. troops in Afghanistan. It's more likely that I will win the next Powerball than the results of these situations will be favorable.

Human Resource Management Practices/Organizational Culture: The importance of HR practices in any organization stems from its contributory role towards the attainment of organizational effectiveness through the performance of personnel hiring, training, and motivation. It is widely accepted that the extent to which an organization moves closer to its strategic objectives depends, in part, on the degree of alignment of the organization's HR practices to the defined objectives. This presupposes that an organization's HR practices will be professionally carried out. If, however, the outcome from an effort is a good measurement frame of the exercised effort, some of the problems with primary care delivery in nursing homes (as reduced to the provision of ADLs) could be attributed to faulty HR practices. For instance, as noted earlier, the job of a CNA is very stressful and challenging—partly due to the difficulty encountered when providing care for some residents. The CNA assigned to a difficult resident will have to work with the resident for the entire shift, and he or she may not possess the energy to work with a particular resident. Effective stress management techniques only work, for the most part, when the source of stress can be checked—not when it is continuous. My recommended model for the management of nursing homes will provide for the following:

- The HR manager for a facility must, in addition to possessing a college-level education (probably a BA in HR management) or professional certification, be able to show understanding of current trends in the practice of HR management. When hired, he or she must have the ability to benchmark best practices and customize the same in the nursing home environment.

- Where gaps are created between HR policies formulated at corporate level and staffing needs (based on the needs of residents), the facility HR manager must be able to perform the challenging task of maintaining employee motivation. Just saying, "It is the policy" sounds dumb and has a negative effect on the residents.
- In addition to the professional/education requirements, HR units of nursing homes must identify a host of other qualities suitable for performance in any job category. These qualities must be defined in some measurable dimension for assessment during interviews. In today's world of HR practices, there are professional firms that will help craft these yardsticks. The current practice whereby anyone who possesses the required certification and satisfactorily provides answers to interview questions (in addition to passing background and drug tests) is assumed to be capable of doing the job is faulty. This practice must be fixed.
- All assignments of CNAs to the floors must be based on the nature and individual needs of the residents and a corresponding fitness of the aides on the other. For instance, there is nothing wrong with a nursing home admitting residents who are 400 pounds or more. There is everything wrong with that same nursing

home hiring and assigning an aide who can hardly lift a leg of a resident to work with that resident. The practice wherein aides are expected to trade residents only works when a good degree of understanding exists among the aides present on the shift. This understanding among aides cannot be assumed away by management. Facility hiring and scheduling practices, most times, do not guarantee the putting together of "like aides."

The creation of a workplace culture capable of collectively carrying along every employee of a nursing home toward the accomplishment of the main goals is important. Such a culture, to be enthroned by management but employee-based, ensures the commonality of purpose for all (management, staff, residents, and family members) and the contributory role of all and sundry. The primary role of this workplace culture is to foster employee productivity and growth, collaboration, teamwork, and motivation. These are all necessary factors that will enhance the provision of resident-certified primary care delivery services. Though complex, integral parts of this culture are as follows:

- An across-the-board improvement in the compensation packages for CNAs.

- The introduction of performance-based benefits packages for hardworking CNAs. As stressfully demanding as the CNA job is, in a nursing home work environment, there are aides who regularly go the extra mile to get things done. An introduction of a rewards package to benefit the hardworking CNA—and not necessarily friends of facility managers—will boost the morale of the entire in-house CNA constituency.
- A drastic reduction of the rate at which CNAs get written up. The CNA constituency in most nursing homes will agree that there are too many unwarranted instances of employees getting written up by all manner of superiors. A CNA should work with confidence and full control of his or her job—not in constant fear of the witch-hunting disposition of some superiors. Also, the dysfunctional attitude and utterances of some facility managers should be checked. Constant threats such as, "Get out," "The front door is open," and "If you do that again, consider your services terminated" coming from members of facility management is counterproductive. These managers need to learn that, in highly professional work environments, a lopsided resort to authority is likely the least effective tool with which to manage subordinates. This is especially true

when subordinates have ample choices with respect to where they want to work.

- The introduction of employee retention policy is very vital to mitigating falling standards in the care delivery system. I have seen a lot of good CNAs leave a nursing home because they were fired for petty reasons or they were frustrated by the attitude of facility management. Such nursing homes fail to understand that a good worker can only be replaced by another good or better one—not every other employee. Good workers are scarce commodities. For the most part, what makes a worker good are his or her personal attributes, which the worker only temporarily leases to the organization. To the extent that they are not easily replaceable, management should work harder to keep these hardworking CNAs.

- The establishment of effective collaboration between and among different strata of employees must occur. In the nursing home environment, collaboration will be defined as a conscious dethroning of the hitherto upheld superiority of the RN or DON in terms of knowledge. Nursing homes must move toward this new platform, even when it means dismantling or bypassing existing hierarchies. Amabile & Khaire (2008 p106) urged managers to "remember that [they] are not the sole fount of ideas. Be the appreciative audience. Ask the inspiring questions. Allow ideas to bubble up from the workforce. Combat the lone inventor myth. Define 'superstar' as someone who helps others succeed." This rather antiquated grip on power—if and when lessened—will ensure that solutions are reached and those who took part in crafting them possess the fire to make them happen.

Restructuring the CNAs' Work Units/Teams: If anything, my discussions on difficult residents points to the need for a restructuring of the work units of CNAs. For instance, the thirty minutes spent toileting resident J (in Chapter 3) could be judiciously utilized to provide ADLs for two other residents who are less demanding. Similarly, the average time it takes an aide to fetch a Hoyer or sling (and secure the assistance of another aide to prepare a resident who is an assist of two . . . and effect the actual transfer) could have been used by these aides to assist two other residents who require only one aide. It will make better unit management sense to first classify residents on the basis of difficulty (with number of aides required for assistance as the criterion). Because residents who get transferred by means other than a gait belt generally require more than one aide for assistance, changes can be made. It will make for better management to put, say, ten of such residents in a unit and assign the unit to two "right" aides with an accompanying unit differential. As much as possible, residents like resident J should belong to units where other members are generally sedentary, calm, and less demanding.

Other than the provision of ADL-type assistance, the monitoring of residents with high risks of falling and response to frequent call light users should not be the responsibilities of CNAs. As much as possible, the activities department should work around these circumstances. I am not suggesting that CNAs should not answer call lights. The point is, unless a CNA is readily available and not providing care to another resident, a reliance on the very busy CNA to promptly answer all call lights demonstrates the ineffectiveness of nursing homes' primary care delivery system. The practice where officers walk around the hallways in search of an aide to come and attend to a call light request is outright laziness. It must be stopped. What, after all, is teamwork? An assignment of twenty-four to thirty residents to two or three CNAs and a nurse to supervise them? Is team membership defined by just having a coworker? What is wrong with a nurse or nurse manager transferring a resident in need of toileting from the wheelchair to the toilet and requesting an aide to get the resident off the toilet when the latter is done? The I-am-the-nurse-if-you-don't-like-it-go-to-a-nursing-school mentality is not productive.

The central idea behind restructuring the CNAs' work units and composition of work teams is essentially linked to the need for a drastic reduction in residents' wait time. A hard-and-fast method of restructuring work units and constituting work teams may not exist, but the notion that the CNA needs to be freed up to have ample time to continuously provide ADLs to residents can serve as a good guide. Though restructuring of work units, if well done, can lead to the effective utilization of the primary caregiver, teamwork presupposes a good measure of uniformity of purpose and a collection of "fits" as a vehicle for realizing the former.

In the almost-ten years that I have been familiar with the business of primary care delivery to nursing home residents, all other service-oriented businesses have striven to successfully improve on their service delivery times. The utilization of self-service stations, kiosks, and UPS by online sellers, are a few of the examples. One question remains: what have nursing homes been doing, especially in the face of increasing complaints from residents and family members? The time to drop the horsewhip with which the classic director of nursing has chased the CNA around the floor of the nursing home is now. At least the DON will be freed up to think of better ways for the CNA to perform.

Use of Technology: For those who live in the United States, the role of technology in this era is a topic they can discuss with the confidence of a college professor. This is because technology has pervaded and penetrated every facet of national life—from the life of an individual at home to what is done at work, school, day care, and even prisons. The appeal to technology use is founded on its power to enhance quality of life by quickening the pace at which things get done. Ask a user of a "dumb" cell phone, and you will hear how he or she can't wait to acquire a Smartphone. One expects nursing homes that do business in the United States to be sufficiently hooked up with this techno-culture by now.

Surprisingly (though differences exist among different nursing homes), tech use is limited to documentation exercises. And still, the documentation formats are not properly streamlined to allow for a gain in average time spent in most cases. For instance, a CNA in a facility in which computer-based charting/documentation has been introduced spends not less than an hour every shift satisfying the documentation requirements. This same exercise probably took fifteen minutes prior to the change from the ledger-type documentation to the new system. The time spent by the CNA for this charting exercise now takes away from the total that should have been devoted to core resident care activities. As important as the charting/documentation exercise is to the entire care delivery system, needed time for primary care delivery activities should not be spent by the CNA providing answers to operationally useless and repetitive questions. For example, it's irrelevant to note whether a non-ambulatory, wheelchair-bound resident walked and the distance walked.

The use of appropriate computer-based technology can solve some of the problems nursing homes face daily. Right at the front desk, visitors should be able to be directed to the room number and floor of the resident they are there to see. Also, facility dietary services and nursing departments should, upon admission of a resident, be on the same page in terms of which diet classification group the resident falls into. There have been frequent instances when, in the dining room, dietary assistants and CNAs did not know what to serve a new resident. Similarly, the voice recording of a beloved family member attached to a sensor alarm can be useful. These recordings can urge the resident to sit or remain lying down and wait for help as the alarm goes off. This will help manage falls. One cannot place an order through a Smartphone in St.

Paul for pizza to be delivered to an address in Minneapolis in a shorter period of time than it would take for a nurse to call from one floor to another to get needed information on a resident. Wondering whether she could obtain the needed information from her work station? A lesson in nursing home 101 may stop you from pondering.

The five component parts discussed in this chapter, sum up my prescribed model for the effective management of a nursing home. The timely provision of ADLs by CNAs to residents is used as a basis for measurement. Most nursing homes have existed under a tradition of practices variously described in the preceding chapters of this book. There is ample reason to believe that these nursing homes will likely continue on the path of existing tradition because, as it is sagely said, "Traditions die hard." The traditional practices of nursing homes stand in the way of my prescription. This means that, for this prescription to become the new norm in nursing homes, sufficient parts of the old must give way. I do, however, recommend additional external regulation of the practices of nursing homes as this transition takes place. Again, the intended outcome from the suggested external regulation could be achieved by nursing homes on their own (through a combination of CNA and resident-friendly managerial practices). The degree to which nursing homes have failed partly necessitates the call for regulation.

Regulating Nursing Homes

All professionals working in nursing homes are known to satisfactorily meet the requirements of their trades at the time of their employment. Also, various states' departments of health have provided an array of checklists with which to monitor the operations of nursing homes. In my opinion, either the content of all existing regulations or the monitoring to ensure compliance have not produced the kind of nursing home environment where the primary reasons for the former's existence could be said to be effectively met. The point is hereby made that the regulation of nursing homes contemplated in this section must be seen in concrete forms sufficient enough to impose a moral duty on nursing home managers toward its residents and caregivers. I am not arguing that all nursing home managers should be morally upright. Rather, I am suggesting that nursing home managers should, at the bare minimum, know and implement what is morally proper for the residents. Resident care is a morally laden exercise, and compassionate care does not come forth from a stone—it proceeds from knowing what is morally right or wrong. What is morally right must therefore be manifested in nursing homes. Pending the arrival of a concrete, comprehensive, and realistic moral frame of expectations for nursing home managers (to be put in place by appropriate governmental departments), an immediate recourse to the following won't hurt:

- Adopting a CNA to residents' ratio of 1:4.
- Holding all nursing home managers (administrators) liable for noncompliance.
- Requiring that all CNAs report shortfalls in staffing (given the 1:4 ratio) through existing resident abuse hotlines. Various departments of health must daily check for compliance—not just during the normal once-a-year surveys.
- Ensuring that only trained medication assistants (TMAs) are used for med passes, freeing up nurses to better do their job.
- Making sure departments of health determine workable equipment-to-residents ratios and hold facility management liable for noncompliance. For instance, a floor with ten residents with the Hoyer/EZ stand as a means of transfer should never work with just one piece of equipment. It is also absurd for a nursing home in twenty-first century America to be without enough workable thermometers.

- Placing at least one functional scale on every floor. The practice of moving a resident from the third floor to the first floor just to take the resident's weight must be stopped immediately.
- Checking that heating and cooling systems are always functional.
- Providing all nursing homes with a deadline for changing all residents' beds to the modern, electric-powered ones used in hospitals.

Conclusion

The model that has been prescribed in this chapter derives from the extensive discussions on the selected themes as they pertain to the nursing home environment. The nursing home's sole business is to provide constant needed care to the adult and aged members of society in a live-in environment. These residents, due to the level of their dependence on others (primarily the CNA), need to be cared for with deep concern, attention, and compassion. It is only logical that any system or style of management designed to provide care for nursing home residents neatly synchronizes with their state of being. A good beginning point would be ensuring that management thinking in nursing homes (as translated into policies) encapsulates this state of being. This will result in the necessary CNA-friendly style of care delivery management—one this chapter has labored to articulate so far, and one that will put the nursing home well on its way to the desired end state.

Bibliography/References

Amabile, T. M & Khaire, M (2008).Creativity and the Role of the Leader. Harvard Business Review, October, 2008, 100-109

Bahrampour, T.(2009). Senior Centers, Nursing Homes Respond to Increased Diversity of Older Population. Washington Post, August 26, 2009. Retrieved online on 5/24/2012

Berfield, S.(2010). C. K. Prahalad, 1941-2010. Bloomberg Businessweek Magazine, April 22, 2010 retrieved online

Doherty, B. Vulnerable Adult Act Review, retrieved online from MDH's website

Jeong, S., & Keatinge, D. (2004). Innovative leadership and management in a nursing home. Journal of Nursing

Management, 12(6), 445-451. doi: 10.1111/j.1365-2834.2004.00451.x

Khurana, R & Nohria, N (2008) It's time to make management a true profession. *Harvard Business Review,* October, 2008, 70-77

Minnesota Department of Health (2007). Your Rights Under The Combined Federal and Minnesota Residents Bill of Rights. Minnesota Department of Health (MDH), July 1, 2007.

Minnesota Department of Health. Comparison of Federal and State Requirements/Definitions.

Minnesota Department of Health. Vulnerable Adult Law and Practice: Section Two, Review of Facts.

MRCI Online Training Center (2012). Vulnerable Adult Training Quiz—2012

National Center on Elder Abuse. Prevention of Abuse and Neglect in Long Term Care Settings. Retrieved from NCEA website on 3/21/2012.

Shafritz, J. M & Hyde, A. C. (2012).From Affirmative Action to Affirming Diversity. In Shafritz & Hyde (Eds.), Classics of Public Administration, Seventh edition (pp. 497-504). Wadsworth Cengage Learning, Boston, USA

Smith, K., & Baughman, R. (2007). Caring for America's aging population: a profile of the direct-care workforce. Monthly Labor Review. September 2007, 20-26.

Society For Human Resource Management (SHRM) Workplace Diversity Series Part 1: Moving Forward With Diversity. Fast Fact. Retrieved online

Vinson, L. D. (2011). Race, Power, & Workforce Diversity: Awareness, Perceptions, & Experiences among Nursing Home leaders. A master's degree thesis submitted to the Department of Psychology, University of Alabama, Tuscaloosa, Alabama, USA.

www.ingramcontent.com/pod-product-compliance
Lightning Source LLC
Chambersburg PA
CBHW030800180526
45163CB00003B/1109